# Imperialism and Canada, 1895-1903

Robert J. D. Page

*Canadian History Through the Press Series*

General Editors:

David P. Gagan, Anthony W. Rasporich

Holt, Rinehart and Winston of Canada Limited

Toronto : Montreal

Distributed in the United States of America by Winston Press

To K. L. and C. D. but for whom this volume
would have appeared much earlier

# The Saturday Globe.

154

LVI, NUMBER 15,824    TORONTO, SATURDAY, NOVEMBER 3, 1900.    PRICE FIVE CENTS

ONE FLAG, ONE ARMY, ONE COUNTRY.

"SIR WILFRID LAURIER IS TOO ENGLISH FOR ME."—Sir Charles Tupper.

# Editors' Preface

Newspapers are widely accepted by historians as useful vehicles of contemporary opinion. In a nation such as Canada, historically dependent on books and periodicals imported from Great Britain and the United States as the principal disseminators of informed opinion, the local daily or weekly newspaper has been almost the sole medium of information and attitudes. And the proliferation of Canadian newspapers since the early decades of the nineteenth century has created for students of Canadian history a vast reservoir of opinion reflecting the political, social, cultural, linguistic, religious and sectional diversity of our country. The *Canadian History Through the Press* series is an attempt to tap this reservoir by reproducing a cross section of journalistic opinion on major issues, events and problems of the Canadian past.

Using the press as a vehicle for the study of history has already been done with some success in the French series, *Kiosk*, which examines public issues and popular culture in volumes ranging from the Dreyfus affair to French cinema. *Canadian History Through the Press* is not quite so ambitious a venture; but it does aim to introduce the student to events which were compelling subjects of discussion for Canadians through the medium in which public discussion most frequently took place. At its best, the Canadian press is a rich source of historical controversy, providing the historian with a sense of the excitement and contentiousness of contemporary issues. Newspaper editors like William Lyon Mackenzie, George Brown, Henri Bourassa and George McCullagh were themselves often at the centre of the political stage or were, like J.W. Dafoe of the Winnipeg *Free Press,* Joseph Atkinson of the Toronto *Star* and Gérard Pelletier of *La Presse* pundits whose voices were carefully heeded by national and local politicians. This is merely one example of the power of the press; but whatever the subject—Confederation, the Quiet Revolution, social reform, foreign policy or pollution—the press has operated (in Marshall McLuhan's words) as a "corporate or collective image [that] demands deep participation."

As editors of *Canadian History Through the Press* we are committed to the idea that students should be introduced to the study of Canadian history through contemporary documents from the very outset. The newspaper is a familiar, and therefore comfortable medium for the novice historian. We have chosen to use it exclusively, fully aware of the limitations of the press as an historical source. When a prominent Canadian politician observed recently that his colleagues spent much of their time "quoting yesterday's newspaper" he was acknowledging the power of the press not merely to reflect, but to dictate opinion. And Will Rogers' caricature of the man who "only knew what he read in the paper" is an equally cogent reminder that newspapers should not be used exclusively as a weathercock of opinion. The student, then, must and inevitably will come to grips with both the limitations and the advantages of newspapers as sources of history. In this respect, our series is also aimed at introducing the student to one of the historian's most crucial problems, that of discriminating between conflicting accounts and interpretations of historical events.

The volumes currently planned for the *Canadian History Through the Press* series embrace topics ranging from the War of 1812 to the Quiet Revolution of the 1960's, from economic history to religious issues. While it is not immediately possible, we hope that in time the series will eventually embrace an even wider spectrum of subjects which permit us to sample not merely the thrust, but the quality of Canadian life.

David P. Gagan,
Anthony W. Rasporich,
May, 1972.

# Preface

Assembling this volume presented a number of editorial problems, for the term "Imperialism" defies precise and scholarly definition. As the following documents demonstrate, it meant very different things to different Canadians and the ideas overlapped separate areas of political, economic, and intellectual history. It is thus difficult to catalogue imperial opinion under a few concrete headings. Furthermore, the problem of space within a single volume necessitated concentrating on some topics and excluding others. In making this selection I have attempted to ensure that the material would be as representative as possible, reflecting both geographic and political differences of opinion. But the major dailies of Toronto and Montreal tended to dominate press discussion. Their greater resources allowed wider news coverage and more penetrating editorial analysis. These journals, therefore, have provided the greatest number of excerpts for this volume. As copies of some newspapers no longer exist, I was unable to consult all the sources I would have liked to include. For instance, most of the radical and labour journals were never preserved by any library or archives.

I cannot conclude this brief preface without a note of thanks to the many individuals and institutions who helped to guide me to the various sources. The staff of the National Library and the Parliamentary Library in Ottawa; the Douglas Library, Queen's University, Kingston; the Bata Library, Trent University, Peterborough; the Toronto Reference Library, the Public Archives of Ontario, and the Anglican Church Archives, Church House, Toronto were all particularly considerate in handling my many requests. Finally, I owe a very special debt to my long suffering secretary, Carol Sherman, who spent many long hours typing and proof-reading the manuscript.

R.J.D.P.
October, 1971

Robert J. D. Page is Associate Professor of History at Trent University, Peterborough, Ontario.

David P. Gagan, general editor of the *Canadian History Through the Press Series,* is Assistant Professor of History at McMaster University, Hamilton, Ontario.

Anthony W. Rasporich, general editor of the *Canadian History Through the Press Series,* is currently Assistant Professor of History at the University of Calgary, Alberta.

# Contents

# Introduction

The documents in this volume attempt to illustrate the range and the depth of Canadian public opinion on "the Empire" at the turn of the twentieth century during the Age of Imperialism. It is important for Canadians to ponder the implications of this earlier era when Canada exhibited strong support for an imperial creed and when the issues presented in the documents dominated Canadian politics, producing a national debate which reached its peak during the Boer War, 1899-1902. Although the intensity and the idealism of the imperialist movement gradually waned, the myths and the mutual suspicions that it created among English and French Canadians remained to threaten the fragile links of national unity. In short, the issues and ideas that evolved from the debate over "imperialism" have had a permanent impact on the evolution of society and politics in twentieth century Canada.

The historian must use this word imperialism with scholarly care, caution, and even a little scepticism. It is one of those "masked words", as John Ruskin sagely observed. Its meaning is unclear and it is usually invoked with heavy emotional overtones. It is often employed to express a whole set of personal beliefs, national characteristics, or, in some cases, even international prejudices. Today the word is used most frequently to convey an idea of international exploitation, but it did not always have such a pejorative connotation. For example, the word imperialism now conjures up an image for some of foreign domination of the Canadian economy. But seventy-five years ago "imperialism" was synonymous with what for many Canadians was an essential part of being Canadian – pride in being associated with the British Empire and subscribing to the idea and the ideals of British imperialism. This volume attempts to document the latter, not the former.

These documents clearly demonstrate that imperialism was both an international and an indigenous movement for Canadians. Some of the concepts characteristic of imperialistic thought, for example, the idea of the "White Man's Burden", were common right across Western Europe and the English-speaking world. Other ideas, such as a British imperial common market, appealed especially to Canadians who adopted it to suit the particular needs of the Canadian economy. Still other ingredients were totally Canadian in origin – for instance the Loyalist myth and the campaign against imperial federation. Thus, Canadian imperialism was a strange collection of disparate ideas and feelings; and this very diversity and ambiguity gave the movement much of its strength for it could appeal to different groups in the community for differing reasons. The student of History must therefore attempt to understand the idea of imperialism in its many complexities, rather than searching for any single thread or idea which runs through the creed of all Canadian imperialists. In Section I of the documents some of these differing views are presented.

For English-speaking Canada, the Empire engendered a fierce pride which engulfed most aspects of public life. It exhibited its most intense form in the popular press, but also found expression in the novels, poetry, economics, philosophy, and sermons of the era. It concentrated in a single focus many of the ideals and aspirations of Victorian Canada. The ethical and religious overtones of the movement gave it a strength and a certainty of purpose seldom found in political movements. Three main ingredients comprised the philosophic base of Canadian imperialism: the English-Canadian commercial-entrepreneurial creed; the country's British political traditions and institutions; and the spiritual zeal of Canadian evangelicalism.

In the first of these traits, one sees the profound Canadian belief in the positive advantages of entrepreneurial capitalism in action. Many Canadians believed that it was these skills which had built the Canadian Pacific Railway and forged Canada into a viable political and economic unit. These ideas are illustrated in document 7 of Section I (Canadian Salute to the Ideals of Cecil Rhodes) and in Section II, which demonstrates the wide Canadian enthusiasm for imperial commercial projects. The Canadian Manufacturers Association supported many of these proposals. They hoped the whole economic structure of the empire would be revitalized by the vigorous action of Canadian businessmen and in time Canada with her resources and skills would become the economic heart of the empire.

Behind the whole imperial movement in Canada was a profound respect for British political institutions and principles. But here as well, one finds very distinctive Canadian adaptations. Free of the class inhibitions of the motherland, Canadians believed they had evolved a purer strain of British political ideals. In the vigorous climate and the free atmosphere of the northern half of North America, liberty and stability had achieved a near perfect balance. Free from European militarism or American "boss rule" democracy, the Canadian pattern could provide the dynamic political creed for the empire as a whole. Such naive romantic visions helped to fire imperial zeal and Canadian pride.

The third of the underlying concepts – the missionary ethic – turned a political movement into a holy crusade. Here the Canadian Protestant denominations played a crucial role by their evangelical crusade to convert Africa, India, and China. The churches that sent workers took a new interest in these areas and in seeing British control established. These churches gave strong public support to Chamberlain's militant policy in South Africa; and George Monro Grant, former moderator of the Presbyterian Church and Principal of Queen's University, called on Canada to send troops to China when the Boxer Rebellion threatened the lives and the work of Canadian missionaries.[1] The spiritual, humanitarian, and political elements in the movement combined to form a potent mixture. The "White Man's Burden" was neither so heroic nor imperial motives quite so idealistic as the stories in the Canadian English-language press portrayed. Yet if in our age of doubt it is easy to be cynical of these men and their ideals, still we cannot understand or appreciate Victorian man by such cynicism. Many were sincerely convinced that they possessed the means, and that they had a divine mission, to convert the world. Proud, presumptuous, and naive the Victorians may have been, but few were charlatans. Many believed that man was perfectable and that the British Empire was the greatest secular force working towards Christian goals.

One of the local ingredients in the Canadian movement was the Loyalist myth, which is outlined in the first document by Sir John Bourinot, a leading Canadian constitutional expert and historian. English Canada had been founded after the American revolution by Loyalist refugees whose essential political characteristics were their professed belief in the unity of the Empire and their hatred of revolution. They transmitted to English-speaking Canada a strong conservative and imperial focus for its early political culture. Not surprisingly, many of the leading figures in the imperial movement of the eighteen-nineties were of United Empire Loyalist stock, men and women with deep family traditions of reverence for Queen and empire. In many books, articles, and school lessons, they portrayed the hardships and the perseverance of the early Loyalists as evidence of Canada's historical commitment to the preservation of the imperial connexion. Thus Canadian history itself was used as an active agent to fire imperial enthusiasm.

The "Idea of Progress" was another article in the imperialists' credo. Many Canadians, such as the writer of document 2 in Section I, believed that the expansion of the British empire would provide a vast umbrella of peace and security under which the world could move forward to new heights of culture, prosperity, and international morality. Because British political principles were sound, the empire could provide the necessary objective arbitration to settle international disputes while the unchallenged power of the Royal Navy would ensure acceptance. More to the point, as Canada inevitably rose to become the most powerful unit in the empire, she would take an increasingly greater role in this process. Thus the imperial road seemed to some Canadians as a certain route to world influence that the Dominion could never achieve on her own.

Quite apart from their idealism, Canadians were drawn to the idea of imperial unity by a number of pragmatic and material considerations. Some Canadians argued that Canada benefitted from the influence and the prestige of British diplomacy and the international diplomatic machinery of the British Foreign Office. Similarly, it was argued that the power of Her Majesty's Armed Forces provided a strong deterrent to potential acts of aggression against Canada. Finally, there was a whole series of imperial economic advantages which Canadians hoped to expand and exploit: British loans for Canadian development, subsidized steamship lines, preferential tariffs in imperial markets, and colonial and war contracts for Canadian companies. These items represented some of the practical and profitable advantages of the British connection which Laurier and other Canadians worked to increase.

It has often been assumed that the imperial movement in Canada represented a retrograde phase in the march to self-government and a fully autonomous Dominion status. Some observers have assumed that behind the movement was a feeling of deference and subservience to mother Britain. This interpretation is shattered by an examination of Canadian attitudes to imperial federation. Canadian imperialists were the most vigorous opponents of the schemes for political centralization of the Empire put forward by Joseph Chamberlain and others in the United Kingdom. Sir Charles Tupper, a zealous imperialist, proudly boasted of having helped to destroy the Imperial Federation League when it attempted to put forward a program for an imperial political federation. The preservation of Canadian autonomy and liberty was a fundamental prerequisite for the future of Canada within the Empire. Imperialism was necessarily tempered by Canadian nationalism.

Anglo-American relations provided another component in both Canadian and British imperialism but in profoundly different ways. In Great Britain, several decades of Anglo-American antagonism had given way, by 1896, to strong feelings of Anglo-Saxon racial affinity with their cousins in the United States, and Britons hoped to forge, eventually, an English-speaking alliance between the two countries to dominate the world. Canadians, as document 17 of Section I illustrates, took quite a different view of the desirability of a close alliance with the United States of America. They viewed their own history largely as the product of American hostility and they wished to build strong imperial links to balance the threat of continentalism. British imperialists reached out for an accord with the United States while Canadian exponents reached out to the empire in order to keep "Uncle Sam" at arm's length.

\*　　　\*　　　\*

Imperial sentiment in Canada was brought to its most excited, feverish pitch by the Boer War. As the Spanish-American War had aroused the United States so the South African War stirred Canadians. The details of the African dispute have long been forgotten in Canada, but they deserve a brief review for an understanding of the documents in this volume. The Boer War was an outgrowth of the struggle among the great powers of Europe for international supremacy which produced the partition of Africa in the period between the late eighteen-seventies and the end of the century. For Britain, the two focal points of strategic interest in Africa were the Nile valley in the north and the Cape colony in the south where the Afrikaans-speaking Boers, descendants of early Dutch colonists, had been engaged in a long struggle to preserve their culture from assimilation through contact with the English-speaking population.

The Boers had migrated from the British coastal colonies to the interior where they had established two pastoral republics, the Orange Free State and the Transvaal, free from British control. Unfortunately, the mining of diamonds on the border of the Orange Free State in the eighteen-seventies and then the discovery of gold in the Transvaal in the eighteen-eighties, attracted British settlers and capitalists who soon demanded a voice in the political affairs of the Boer republics. The Transvaal Republic was not prepared, however, to grant political rights to these aliens or *uitlanders*. Cecil Rhodes therefore deliberately fomented discontent to try to force the British government to intervene. The ill-considered and foolhardy filibustering raid by Dr. Jameson and his Bechuanaland police in December 1895, designed to precipitate a crisis, poisoned relations between the two groups and raised the tension between the British government and the Transvaal. Britain claimed suzerainty over the Transvaal and therefore responsibility for improving the position of the *uitlanders*. The militant British Colonial Secretary, Joseph Chamberlain, sparred with Paul Kruger, the intransigent President of the Transvaal, in a lengthy and bitter diplomatic dispute which brought both countries to the brink of war early in the fall of 1899. Kruger chose to act first; he issued an ultimatum to Britain and invaded British territory barely in advance of a similar move by Britain.

In Canada, the South African situation had not been followed closely; not even the Jameson Raid provoked much interest. However, as tension mounted in 1899, the imperial feeling of English-speaking Canada, which was already strong, now burst forth in fiery rhetoric for the British cause in South Africa. While French Canada looked on without interest, English Canada worked itself into an emotional frenzy which exceeded all normal bounds when the Boers invaded British territory to start the war. Liberals and Conservatives united in the chorus demanding that Canadian troops be sent to aid the imperial forces.

Laurier at first rejected the idea of sending troops, reflecting the previous policy of John A. Macdonald who had opposed sending forces to the Sudan in 1885. But he finally bowed to public pressure and permitted a contingent of volunteers to be raised for service in South Africa. Even so, many Canadians remained dissatisfied. On one side, some French-Canadian members of his party, including Israel Tarte (Minister of Public Works) and Henri

6

Bourassa (M.P. for Labelle) as well as a small group of French-Canadian nationalists opposed Canadian participation. On the other side, the imperialists of English Canada denounced Laurier for being so slow to act. Moreover, because the opposition to participation seemed to be solely from French Canada, ethnic tensions intensified partisan differences. The government was denounced for its French domination and its disloyalty to Britain. Those deep anti-French, anti-Catholic passions which had been aroused by Riel and the Manitoba Schools Issue now found a new focus on the issue of sending troops to South Africa.

As the documents in this volume illustrate clearly, these tensions produced some of the wildest and most irresponsible journalism in the history of Canada. Even a staunch imperialist like Lord Minto, the Governor-General, was appalled by the ravings of some of the Ontario papers. He wrote to his brother in England:

> The writing of the leading opposition papers has been positively wicked—simply aiming at stirring up hatred of French Canada—so much so that Ontario farmers the other day were actually going to bed with loaded rifles and revolvers by their sides for fear of the French! It is perfectly monstrous.... The French papers have been more moderate than the English ones...the race feeling is running very high and there is much wild talk.... I believe that the French Canadians are very much maligned as to their disloyalty. French Canada does not wish to be mixed up in Imperial Wars and is lukewarm, but at home apparently you do not call a man disloyal if he disapproves of the war—here if he is only lukewarm and is a French Canadian he must be a rebel ... that is the British bulldog argument here.[2]

The Hamilton *Spectator*, the Toronto *News*, and the Toronto *Mail and Empire* were three of the worst offenders. Had Britain achieved a quick victory in South Africa these tensions might have eased greatly. But the first months of the war saw a series of British reverses which prompted some French Canadians to cheer for the outgunned and outnumbered Boers. That drove many English Canadians into a desperate state of mind. The Montreal student riots described below were a product of the deepening conflict between the imperialist and nationalist factions.

The leading figure in the French Canadian nationalist faction was Henri Bourassa, the brilliant and eloquent Member of Parliament for Labelle, who broke with Laurier over sending the troops to South Africa, an action that he regarded as a revolution in Canada's constitutional relationship with Britain; and he developed an elaborate theory of conspiracy to explain Canada's involvement. To save Britons from military conscription, London was attempting to entice the self-governing colonies into raising troops for every imperial war. At the base of this conspiracy was both the British Government and the Rhodes' mining interests in South Africa. The latter controlled the press reports coming from Africa and even sent agents to Ottawa to influence Canadian politicians and public opinion. Chamberlain and the British government added to this pressure by ordering British officials such as the Governor-General and the militia commander to push reluctant but weak Canadian politicians such as Laurier into military commitments that were contrary to the national interests of the Dominion. Chamberlain found many willing allies in the English-Canadian press as owners and editors hungered for imperial honours or favours.

Such was Bourassa's explanation of Canadian participation. But he also denounced the materialism and the militarism of the imperial movement as characteristics that should be excluded as far as possible from Canadian society. Bourassa's arguments, which reflect the nationalists' debt to such radical British opponents of imperialism as J. A. Hobson and the bitterly anti-British Parisian press, represent the rational basis of the nationalists' opposition to imperial unity. But undoubtedly much of their fervour was provoked, not by the events taking place in Africa, but by the press of Ontario. In Section III of this volume, their ethnic and religious prejudices emerge very clearly. It was hardly surprising, therefore, that some in Quebec viewed imperialism as a further vehicle for the cultural assimilation of French Canada. The primary responsibility for this ethnic feud must rest with those Ontario journals that were so quick to impugn the motives of French Canadians.

\*       \*       \*

Because of the tensions created by the Boer War, the military aspects of imperialism have tended to preoccupy historians. However, in the period 1896-1902 Canadians were equally concerned with the economic and constitutional implications of the idea of imperial unity, particularly with the economic potential of the Empire as a market for Canadian goods.

Until the repeal of the Corn Laws in the eighteen-forties, Canadian goods had enjoyed preferential entry into the British market. When this preference was ended, Canadians turned south to the United States and in 1854 a reciprocity agreement allowed a free flow of natural products. Partly due to the demands of a war economy in the United States, the early eighteen-sixties were boom years for Canadians which ended abruptly when the Americans terminated the agreement in 1866. Confederation was partly an attempt to create an integrated British North American market to replace the United States. The succeeding decades, however, were far from prosperous. Canadian hopes for a new reciprocity agreement with the Americans seemed dashed when Washington turned sharply protectionist in the eighteen-nineties. In any case the 1891 election showed that Canadians then, as now, were worried about the political implications of closer economic ties with the United States.

Consequently, rising imperial sentiment and the particular needs of the Canadian economy to expand the market for export staples, led Canadians to reconsider the importance of their economic ties with Britain. Those who saw the Empire as the logical field for Canadian economic activity argued in favour of a system of imperial tariff preferences that would give Britain, the Dominions and the colonies trading advantages in each other's markets by building tariff barriers against non-imperial products. The political advantages for Laurier and the Liberals were obvious. The measure would meet the demands of electors for tariff reform to promote freer trade, and would appear at the same time to be a major economic step towards the nebulous goal of imperial unity. In addition tariff protection against American manufactures would be maintained. Such a scheme became vital to Canada as settlers began to pour into the west in the late eighteen-nineties and new markets for Canadian grain became imperative. A reciprocal tariff preference would help Canada secure the British market for grain from Russian, American, and Argentinian competition and ensure the future prosperity of the prairies and the Dominion as a whole.

In 1897 Canada took the first step unilaterally by offering a tariff reduction to British goods entering Canada. Later this was expanded to include some of the other colonies. But it was very difficult for Britain to offer anything in return. Any preferential scheme would have forced Britain to abandon free trade, and thus would have forced up the price of food for the average working man in the United Kingdom. Nevertheless, as a sign of his good faith, Joseph Chamberlain carried the scheme through the Balfour cabinet in the fall of 1902, but he left for his extended reconstruction tour of South Africa before it was made public in the budget. In the three months he was gone the free trade elements regained the ascendancy in cabinet and he returned to hear a budget which dashed his hopes. In September 1903 he resigned from the government to lead a personal campaign in the country that eventually failed. It was not until the Ottawa agreements of 1932 that even a limited scheme of multilateral imperial preferences was instituted.

The Fielding imperial preferential tariff was a curious extension of much of the economic thinking involved in Macdonald's National Policy which had been designed to promote western settlement, protect eastern manufactures, and strengthen the trans-continental railway. Now, in the era of imperial unity, the Canadian Pacific hoped to become the great imperial highway for civilian and military traffic between Britain and her Pacific possessions. The Canadian Manufacturers' Association supported imperial preference because, while maintaining protection on American manufactures, it offered the hope of further markets in Australia, Britain, and South Africa. Also the campaign for imperial unity might help to deflect northward the flow of British immigrants to the United States. These families would be settled in the west to increase the market for eastern manufactures and traffic for the railway. If Britain offered a reciprocal preference, the east-west transportation links would be strengthened even further.

Thus, in Canada, economic imperialism was closely linked to Canadian aspirations for the economic development of the country. Strong imperial ties made it easier and cheaper to borrow on the London money market, and allowed Canadian businesses to bid for contracts let by the British government or army. Imperial communications projects such as a subsidized intercolonial steamship service were seen as an extension of the objectives of the "National Policy" to the wider field of the empire. For these and other reasons, many prominent Liberals, such as Premier Ross of Ontario, pressed Laurier for imperial commercial cooperation. In sum, imperial sentiment in Canada was not determined by economic factors, but it was deeply influenced and strengthened by them.

\*       \*       \*

The Boer War, imperial preferential trade, and the national debate over the nature and meaning of the imperial relationship provided the background for the colonial conference that convened in London in the summer of 1902. There, the discussions revolved around Joseph Chamberlain's proposals for a military federation of the Empire, which would commit the colonies to a compulsory role in the defence of the Empire. Laurier emerged as the chief antagonist to this scheme, arguing that Canadian participation in imperial military ventures must be decided on the justice of each case as it arose. Most Canadians applauded Laurier's stand. In spite of their zeal for the British position in South Africa, Canadians wished to avoid involvement in a European war. Nor did Canadians wish to be forced into military preparedness by the dictates of outside authority. Twice during these years two senior imperial officers, General Hutton and Lord Dundonald, were forced to resign as General-Officers Commanding the Canadian Militia for pursuing military development in Canada more zealously than government policy or popular opinion warranted.

In the end, the Colonial Conference failed to produce any agreement on the question of closer imperial unity, largely due to Laurier's vigorous defence of Canadian autonomy. Thereafter, imperial preferential trade held out the only meaningful prospect of imperial cooperation, but Britain's commitment to free trade frustrated Chamberlain's tariff proposals. By 1903, the idea of imperial federation was a dead issue.

\*       \*       \*

The enthusiasm of Canadians for imperialism did not mean, as many British statesmen assumed, that Canadians desired a redefinition of the imperial relationship such as a military or political federation of the Empire might entail. Canadians wanted the glory and the benefits of Empire while avoiding the costs and obligations. They saw the Empire as a means of achieving a new status, which, as an independent nation, they could never attain. Empire was their entrance to the world stage; but at the same time they wished to preserve Canadian autonomy. Just as American chauvin-

11

ism found its outlet in Cuba and the Philippines, Canadians stressed Canada's important role in the progress of British imperialism. In this way they tried to enhance national prestige.

English Canada viewed the Empire as essential to the building of a powerful and influential "British" nation in North America. Here we find an interesting early form of Canadian nationalism. Canadian troops were sent to South Africa to demonstrate Canada's new strength and aspirations. As the first contingents of Canadian troops ever sent from her shores, their progress and achievements were followed with great pride in the columns of the popular press. Laurier himself illustrated something of Canada's exaggerated feeling of importance when he commented on the news of the Battle of Paardeberg in the House of Commons: "is there a man whose bosom did not swell with pride ... the pride of the consciousness that that day the fact had been revealed to the world that a new power had arisen in the west."[3]

The Boer War was the great high-water mark of imperial zeal in Canada. But the war brought with it the seeds for the weakening of imperial sentiment. The final two years of fighting were confined to the brutality and frustrations of a guerilla campaign, which were hardly consistent with the idealistic rhetoric of earlier years. Imperial feeling carried on after 1902 but it never regained that certainty of sacred purpose, which it exhibited in 1899. Especially with the results of the Alaska Boundary Award in 1903 Canadians became more realistic in their attitudes to international and imperial affairs. Some of the zeal remained, but the wild excesses of the early months of the Boer War were not repeated until 1914-18.

Ultimately the significance of Canadian imperialism was not that it stimulated elements of nationalism but rather that it perpetuated and intensified the split between the two developing nationalisms of Canada. Lacking a revolutionary tradition, Canada was faced with the problem of building unifying bridges which would join the national attitudes and aspirations of her two founding cultures. The excesses and prejudices involved in the imperial patriotism of English Canada postponed the possibility of building those bridges and widened the gap they had to span. Although the nationalism of English Canada developed out of imperial enthusiasm and that of French Canada in opposition to it, they still had many other interests in common. In the aftermath of the Boer War these common interests were lost from view. Regrettably the Canadian press must assume considerable responsibility for this weakening of the fragile unity of the country.

In the long history of Canadian journalism, few issues have excited the press and population as did imperialism. Many English-Canadian editors were leading exponents of empire and their newspapers reflected their enthusiasm. By purple prose and lofty metaphor they portrayed the Empire as humane, triumphant, and piously motivated. News stories of the sacrificial martyrdom of a missionary evoked all the clichés of the "White Man's Burden". The alleged savagery of African native customs and the horrors of the slave trade were paraded constantly as proof of the need for Christian order and civilization to bring "light" to the "dark" continent. In a period before there was an appreciation of the value of non-Western cultures, it was easy to be contemptuous of all other religious and social patterns. But the Victorian was certain that he had found most of the essentials for liberating human progress. It has taken two world wars and all the butchery of the twentieth century to erode but not eliminate this presumptuous attitude.

With the newly completed intercontinental cable services in the eighteen-nineties news from Africa and Asia flowed into Canadian newspaper offices within hours of the event, whereas before it had taken weeks or even months. These improvements gave Canadians a sense of immediacy they had never experienced before. The scramble for Africa, the Boer War, and the Boxer Rebellion received detailed coverage on a daily basis, which gave these events so much greater impact than the Crimean War or the Indian Mutiny of the eighteen-fifties. In this age of imperialism, the press sparked unprecedented Canadian interest in world affairs, helping to draw the country out of its parochial, nineteenth century North American shell.

For better or worse, sensationalism often played a major role in this process. During the Boer War many wholly fictitious events were described in vivid detail. On the eve of the war the Hamilton *Spectator* carried the story that the Boers had dynamited a refugee train of three hundred women and children fleeing from the Transvaal. Having no foundation in fact, such stories aroused English-Canadian emotions and promoted the irrational war fever that forced Laurier to send troops. The political storm involved in this decision centred on Israel Tarte, Laurier's Minister of Public Works, who had opposed the sending of Canadian troops. As the *Spectator* thundered: "When British women and children are being murdered at wholesale by the Boers, it is high time that the Boers' friend Tarte, was out of the government of a loyal British colony." In addition many of the newspapers took an aggressive, militaristic posture on the issue of the war itself. Weeks before hostilities commenced, some Canadian journals openly called for war. The Ottawa *Citizen* emphatically declared: "It is about time that the Transvaal war demonstrated its inevitability."[4] In this way the Canadian press anticipated and fed the intensity of English Canada's fervour for such a distant war.

It has been assumed that the jingoism of the Canadian press resulted from the dependence on British cable services. In fact most of the overseas news came from American organizations operating through New York City. Only a couple of the wealthiest Toronto and Montreal papers could afford their own cable link to London. John Cooper, editor of the *Canadian Magazine* condemned the Canadian newspapers of 1898 for their dependence on American sources. He wrote bitterly:

> As citizens we often lament the slow growth of patriotism and of Canadian literature. And is this slowness of growth surprising when our newspapers make no difference between what is foreign and what is Canadian ... We seldom see a quotation from a British newspaper in a Canadian daily, unless it is in the cable despatches, and ninety-five per cent of these cables come through New York .... And yet we pride ourselves on our British connection; we revere the Union Jack and all it represents....[5]

It was not until September 1903 that an independent Canadian wire service was established in London. Financed with a grant of $15,000 from the Laurier government, two correspondents became resident in London to telegraph materials back to the Canadian press.[6] Thus for the period of this volume, the British influence on the Canadian press has been exaggerated; and in any case many of the news reports that did originate in London were modified for American consumption even before they reached the Canadian newspaper offices. Therefore, if the press reports from South Africa which were printed in Canada were heavily pro-British, it was due to the imperial patriotism of those Canadian editors who completely ignored the Boer side of the dispute contained in these despatches.

The Canadian press of the eighteen-nineties was more vigorous, more outspoken, and more partisan than the press of today. In 1901 Canadians had a choice of 116 daily newspapers—43 Liberal, 42 Conservative, 30 Independent, and 1 Labour. Halifax had five dailies, Montreal seven, and Toronto six. Smaller cities such as Charlottetown, Kingston, Peterborough, and St. Catharines supported three each – something impossible today. The geographic distribution of these dailies was curiously significant.

| | |
|---|---|
| Maritimes | - 22 |
| Quebec | - 15 (12 in Montreal/Quebec City) |
| Ontario | - 55 |
| Manitoba | - 7 |
| North West Territories | - 1 (at Calgary) |
| British Columbia | - 12 |
| Yukon | - 4 |

The West was still not settled and English Canadians tended to support a daily newspaper more readily than French Canadians. In addition there was a very vigorous weekly press, which was even more extensive as it carried right down to the village level. The English and French religious press was also influential and participated vigorously in the political discussions of the day. However, Canada seems to have lacked a significant radical or labour press. There were a few examples of protest journals such as Goldwin Smith's agrarian *Weekly Sun*. But these constituted a relatively mild form of protest.

The two leading papers in the Imperial crusade were the Liberal Toronto *Globe* and the Conservative Montreal *Star*. The *Globe* under the intelligent editorship of John S. Willison until he moved to the Toronto *News* in 1902, often contained the most thoughtful Canadian comments on imperial affairs. Although a strong imperial supporter it was not as bombastic or jingoistic as Hugh Graham's Montreal *Star*. With intimate links to the Laurier administration the *Globe* was probably the most influential journal in the country and was frequently quoted by other editors. It is fitting, therefore, that it should supply the largest number of excerpts for this volume.

The journals of French Canada exhibited widely differing views on imperialism. *Le Soleil* of Quebec City supported many of the imperial projects including the sending of troops to South Africa. However, this position was hardly surprising as Pacaud, the editor, was a close friend and supporter of Laurier. *La Patrie* and *La Presse* of Montreal both tended to support Laurier's policy but with critical reservations. *Le Temps* of Ottawa and *L'Événement* of Quebec City were strongly critical of imperialism throughout. But the real bitterness and anti-imperialism emerged only from some of the small nationalist weeklies such as Jules-Paul Tardivel's *La Vérité*, an ultramontane journal of Quebec City.

Unlike today, ownership of the Canadian press was fragmented with most papers operating as independent entities. Usually they were locally financed, often by wealthy supporters of a political party. In a few cases outside interests bought control; for instance both the Manitoba *Free Press* and *La Presse* of Montreal were owned for part of this period by railway interests – the former by the Canadian Pacific Railway and the latter by Mackenzie and Mann. Often the owners controlled strictly the editorial policy of their papers. When Joseph Atkinson negotiated relative freedom for himself as the new editor of the Toronto *Star* in 1899, his position was exceptional. Many owners viewed their journals as a personal form of participation in the political struggles of the day. They were not merely observers or analysts. They saw their newspapers as vehicles to expound and convert. To such men moderation and neutrality were viewed as signs of weakness and lack of principle. They believed they were following in the traditions of Joseph Howe, William Lyon Mackenzie, and George Brown as crusading journalists. Such an approach differs markedly from most journalists today.

Canadians were relatively proud of their press, which they believed had avoided the vulgar sensationalism of the American "Yellow" press. But some of the same pressures were at work in Canada. New steam presses turned out greatly increased production runs in less time, thus allowing for the mass circulation dailies. There was fierce competition within the major cities for circulation and the ensuing advertising revenue. To gain circulation they attempted to add colour and drama to their pages. Many papers sent correspondents to South Africa to give the exciting first-hand descriptions of the Canadian troops in action. These were the first war correspondents sent overseas from Canada and extended war coverage boosted circulation for some papers.[8] Nevertheless, the Canadian journals also had a more thoughtful side as exemplified by their expanded Saturday editions in which there appeared "think pieces," book reviews, serious serialized literature and even poetry. For example, Rudyard Kipling had a wide impact on Canadians through these pages.

The Canadian newspaper, closer to the British in tone but strongly American in layout and appearance, was the Victorian Canadian's principal source of "intelligence", and one contemporary observer was led to boast that "in no branch of effort has Canadian progress been more marked than in journalism."[9] Whether the Canadian press deserved such accolades may be judged by the contents of this volume.

## Notes to Introduction

1. Toronto *Globe*, May 15, 1901.

2. Lord Minto to Arthur Eliot, November 25, 1900, Minto Papers, Vol. 36, Public Archives of Canada.

3. Canada, House of Commons, Debates, March 13, 1900, Col. 1848.

4. Hamilton *Spectator*, October 13, 1899; Ottawa *Citizen*, October 2, 1899.

5. John A. Cooper [signed editorial], *The Canadian Magazine* (November, 1898), 81; and see also the Vancouver *Province*, October 28, 1899.

6. John Castell Hopkins, *The Canadian Annual Review, 1903* (Toronto: Annual Review Publishing Company, 1914), p. 563.

7. Ramsay Cook, *The Politics of John W. Dafoe and the Free Press* (Toronto: University of Toronto Press, 1963), p. 15; Ross Harkness, *J. E. Atkinson of the Star* (Toronto: University of Toronto Press, 1963), pp. 46 ff.; W. H. Kesterton, *A History of Journalism in Canada* (Toronto: McClelland and Stewart, 1967), p. 91.

8. Harkness, *op. cit.*, p. 50.

9. Arthur F. Wallis, "A Historical Sketch of Canadian Journalism," in J. C. Hopkins, *Canada: An Encyclopaedia*, 7 vols., (Toronto: Linscott Publishing Company, 1898-1900), Vol. V, p. 182.

# Guide to Documents

## SECTION I  The Ideas and Bonds of Empire

1. The Loyalist Legacy feeds Imperial Enthusiasm. *The Globe,* Toronto, December 4, 1897.

2. The Ideal of Imperialism: Peace and World Progress. *The Globe,* Toronto, January 4, 1902.

3. Humanitarianism: a part of Imperialism? *The Globe,* Toronto, April 7, 1902.

4. Queen Victoria: Her Moral and Social Influence over her Imperial Subjects. *The Star,* Toronto, January 23, 1901.

5. Queen Victoria: living symbol of British Liberty. *The Canadian Churchman,* Toronto, July 1, 1897.

6. The Thrill of British Imperial Expansion in Africa. *The Canadian Magazine,* Toronto, October, 1898.

7. Canadian Salute to the Ideals of Cecil Rhodes. *The Methodist Magazine and Review,* Toronto, January, 1900.

8. Canadian Contribution to the Khartoum Relief Force. *The Morning Chronicle,* Quebec, September 16, 1884.

9. Canadian Hero helps Kitchener retake Khartoum. *The Province,* Vancouver, July 11, 1899.

10. The Coronation of Edward VII: reflections on the universality of the British Empire. *The Examiner,* Peterborough, June 16, 1902.

11. Imperialism as Part of the Divine Plan. *The Orange Sentinel,* Toronto, March 23, 1899.

12. Imperialism and the Missionary Impulse: a case of dissimilar motivations. *The Globe,* Toronto, March 25, 1899.

13. Imperialism and Protestantism: a parallel progress. *The Orange Sentinel,* Toronto, July 27, 1899.

14. Roman Catholics and Loyalty. *The Province,* Victoria, January 23, 1897.

15. Racial Darwinism and Imperialism. *The Canadian Churchman,* Toronto, July 8, 1897.

16. Canada's Duty to the Empire. *The Manitoba Free Press,* Winnipeg, January 6, 1896.

17. Imperialism and Canadian-American Relations. *The Globe,* Toronto, December 6, 1897.

18. Imperial Unity for the Defence of Canada. *The Globe,* Toronto, April 7, 1899.

19. Canadian Self-Confidence: solidarity with the Empire. *The London Advertiser,* September 20, 1900.

20. Canada's Imperial Responsibilities. *The Globe,* Toronto, November 26, 1900.

21. Moral Influence of Canada on the Empire. *The Star,* Montreal, January 22, 1900.

22. Canadian Nationalism and Imperialism. *The London Advertiser,* September 28, 1900.

23. Canada Rejects Imperial Federation. *The Province,* Victoria, March 20, 1897.

24. An English Canadian Dissenting Voice: Imperialism and Social Justice. *The Province,* Victoria, March 6, 1897.

25. A French Canadian Dissenting Voice: Imperialism means bloodshed and taxation. *L'Interprète,* Montebello, Quebec, October 12, 1893.

## SECTION II Unity for Trade: The Imperial Preferences, 1896-1902

1. History of the Idea of Imperial Preference. *The Globe,* Toronto, August 18, 1897.

2. The Conservative Party Supports the Idea. *The Citizen,* Ottawa, May 6, 1896.

3. The Liberal Party Supports Preferential Trade. *The Globe,* Toronto, May 20, 1896.

4. The Flow of British Capital into Canada. *The Star,* Montreal, July 6, 1896.

5. The Advantages of Free Trade. *The Morning Chronicle,* Halifax, January 16, 1897.

6. Laurier's Trade Mission to Washington, 1897. *The Citizen,* Ottawa, February 10, 1897.

7. The Liberals, the Budget and the Coming Tariff. *The Star,* Montreal, April 21, 1897.

8. The New Tariff. *The Globe,* Toronto, April 26, 1897.

9. The New Tariff: a Maritime view. *The Morning Chronicle,* Halifax, April 23, 1897.

10. Conservative Support for the New Tariff. *The Star,* Montreal, April 23, 1897.

11. Liberal Tariff Erases Tory Discrimination. *The Globe,* Toronto, April 23, 1897.

12. Compliments from London. *The Times,* London, April 26, 1897, as quoted in *The Globe,* Toronto, April 27, 1897.

13. Laurier is More English than Canadian. *Le Monde,* Montreal, April 26, 1897.

14. The New Tariff: variation on an old theme. *The Daily Sun,* Saint John, April 26, 1897.

15. Rudyard Kipling Salutes Canada. *The Star,* Montreal, April 28, 1897.

16. Laurier: tool of the Monopolists. *The Weekly Sun,* Toronto, April 29, 1897.

17. Conservative Objections to the Imperial Preference. *The Sarnia Observer,* April 30, 1897.

18. Object of Preferential Tariffs: freer trade. *The Monetary Times,* Toronto, April 30, 1897.

19. The New Tariff proves the loyalty of the Liberal Party. *The Sarnia Observer,* May 7, 1897.

20. Canadian hope for an Empire-wide Preferential Scheme. *The Manitoba Free Press,* Winnipeg, October 8, 1897.

21. Chamberlain and Preferential Trade. *The Star,* Montreal, April 4, 1900.

22. Contracts for Canada: the material benefits of Imperialism. *The Globe,* Toronto, September 1, 1900.

23. A Reply to Conservative Critics of Imperial Preference. *The London Advertiser,* September 21, 1900.

24. Support for an Imperial Trade Federation. *The Globe,* Toronto, February 14, 1901.

25. The Preferential Tariff: an end to colonial autonomy. *La Vérité,* Quebec, April 20, 1901.

26. Laurier's aim: to widen Canada's markets overseas. *Le Soleil,* Quebec, July 9, 1901.

27. A Review of Imperial Relations to 1897. *The Weekly Sun,* Toronto, July 29, 1897.

## SECTION III Canada and the Boer War, 1899-1902

1. Canada Hears of the Jameson Raid. *The Globe,* Toronto, January 1, 1896.

2. Criticism of the British South Africa Company. *The Globe,* Toronto, January 7, 1896.

3. War Spirit. *The Province,* Vancouver, July 3 and 11, 1899.

## SECTION IV   The Colonial Conference of 1902 and its aftermath

# A Note on the Documents

Unless otherwise noted, the documents reproduced below conform, in spelling, grammatical usage and punctuation, to the originals. Since *Canadian History Through the Press* is, in a limited sense, a history of Canadian journalism, it has seemed advisable to preserve contemporary usage however questionable it might appear to be, in order to illustrate the changing quality of Canadian journalistic writing.

# Section I

## The Idea And The Bonds Of Empire

# 1 THE LOYALIST LEGACY FEEDS IMPERIAL ENTHUSIASM

*The Globe, Toronto*
*December 4, 1897*

The *Globe* is here quoting from a speech by Sir John Bourinot (1837-1902), Canadian historian and political scientist. Bourinot was a noted authority on the Canadian Constitution and government.

This Loyalist migration was in many respects one of the most remarkable that ever came into any country. Its members were imbued with many qualities that were calculated to lay deep and firm the foundations of stable institutions, of moral and conservative habits, in the formative period of the Canadian nation's growth. These people were, as some American writers now justly call them, the Unionists of those days, just as the revolutionists were the Secessionists. In other words, they were the champions of a united British Empire in the eighteenth century. They comprised the larger portion of the men and women of culture and wealth throughout the old colonies. As Professor Hosmer has written, the majority "were people of substance and their stake in the country was greater than even that of their opponents, and their patriotism was to the full as fervent." Their estates were among the fairest in the land; they loved beauty, dignity and refinement, but the day went against them and they had to crowd into ships with the gates of their country barred forever behind them.

... no time was more opportune than the present to recall the history of the courageous men and women who more than one hundred years ago, left their homes in the old British Colonies for the sake of a United Empire. The brilliant spectacle that was witnessed on the streets of London in June last, when Canadians joined with representatives from all parts of England's dominions to express their devotion to the Queen, and their attachment to the British connection – a magnificent spectacle of a contented, loyal and united Empire – might well stand out on the broad canvass of history in remarkable contrast with the melancholy picture of the last century, when banks of weeping exiles were seen finding their way to the shores of the possessions that England still owned on the shores of the Atlantic and in the valley of the St. Lawrence .... But though they are no longer here, and even the names of most of them are forgotten, their spirit still survives in the confidence and energy with which the people of this Dominion are laboring to develop the great natural heritage which they possess on the American continent, and in the loyalty which they feel for the British Crown and Empire.

# 2 THE IDEAL OF IMPERIALISM: PEACE AND WORLD PROGRESS

*The Globe, Toronto*
*January 4, 1902*

Imperialism in its last and highest development, imperialism as it possesses and controls the race at the present moment, is not only no breeder of wars, but is the greatest agency for peace the world contains. The period of expansion is over. The work that lies before us is organization, assimilation, development, and material, mental, and moral progress. That is the ideal of our statesmen, an ideal which finds its origin in the best impulses of the race. ... Its great weight and influence must always be on the side of peace; yet we may be sure that wars will come.

# 3 HUMANITARIANISM: A PART OF IMPERIALISM?

*The Globe, Toronto*
*April 7, 1902*

While there has been in the last few years a great deal of discussion about imperialism, there are many evidences that we are as yet only on the threshold of the subject. The discussion has proceeded mainly on the lines of forms of government, commerce, and defence. One question, that of the famine in India, has hardly been dealt with as an imperial question at all. The famine has, of course, attracted the attention of humane people here and elsewhere, and a good deal of assistance has been given. But we do not remember ever to have seen the matter referred to in any imperialist programme, that would appeal to an American as well as a Canadian or an Australian.

## 4  QUEEN VICTORIA: HER MORAL AND SOCIAL INFLUENCE OVER HER IMPERIAL SUBJECTS

*The Star, Toronto*
*January 23, 1901*

The remarks of a Toronto Police Magistrate on the death of Queen Victoria as reported in the *Star*.

In all the long line of those who have ruled over our race, there is not one whose reign will compare, either in greatness of progress or good accomplished throughout the Empire, not only as a constitutional Sovereign and a wise ruler, but also as to the extraordinary influence she has exerted over the ordinary every-day life of her people. She has set a moral example that is something unique in the world's history, an example that has changed the whole ... life of the Empire. . .

## 5  QUEEN VICTORIA: LIVING SYMBOL OF BRITISH LIBERTY

*The Canadian Churchman, Toronto*
*July 1, 1897*

Homage to Queen Victoria at the Diamond Jubilee celebrations in Toronto.

Of our own procession in this the Queen City of Ontario, we were mostly justly proud – proud of the physique, the splendid presence of Canada's sons, proud of our Italian and of our coloured brethren, proud to see the Orange and the Green marching shoulder to shoulder and foot to foot, and by their unanimity doing honour to themselves and to the Sovereign of Britain. A shade of sorrow passes over all. Would to heaven it had been so ordered that the Red Man, once the owner of these fair fields, had been marching too. Alas! he was not present. The hunting grounds are now another's. And now we ask, what is the secret of all this fixed and permanent and devoted passion to Britain's Queen. The reply is at hand. It is the spirit of the British law which makes liberty commensurate with and inseparable from British soil.

## 6  THE THRILL OF BRITISH IMPERIAL EXPANSION IN AFRICA

*The Canadian Magazine, Toronto*
*October, 1898, p. 237*

The wise man may well say "Heaven save us from jingoism," but the calmest pulse can scarcely fail to be quickened at the growth of that red cross on the map of Africa – the approaching arms of steel rails stretching towards each other from the north and south – Cecil Rhodes driving up by the shores of Lake Tanganyika, on the one hand, and Herbert Kitchener hurrying up to Fashoda on the other, while from east and west the other arms of the cross approach to meet in mid-Africa. Let it be hoped that it is a signal of a happy civilization and light for that dark continent that has been the mystery of the ages.

## 7 CANADIAN SALUTE TO THE IDEALS OF CECIL RHODES

*The Methodist Magazine and Review,*
*Toronto*
*January, 1900*

The literature of imperialism is filled with heroes and hero-worship. Here is one example dealing with Cecil John Rhodes: financier, politician, and imperial architect.

Mr. Rhodes occupies no official position in South Africa. He is no soldier, neither is he intrusted with any official or diplomatic functions. But he is still, in war as in peace, the most conspicuous figure on the South African stage.

Mr. Rhodes, finding that war was inevitable, suddenly found himself restless at Cape Town, and, yielding to an uncontrollable impulse, set out for Kimberley on the very eve of its investment by the forces of the Boers. There he is, and there he is likely to remain. He has equipped a force of four hundred men at a cost of £15,000, and cheerfully awaits the development of events. Of the wisdom of placing himself in such an exposed position, almost within grasp of the enemy, it is unnecessary to speak. Mr. Rhodes is not a man who acts upon calculation in such a case, but upon instinct.

Cecil J. Rhodes, a dozen years ago, was unknown outside the narrow confines of the Cape Colony. General Gordon, who had been in South Africa, had met him there sixteen years ago, and formed so high an estimate of his character, that when he started on his heroic mission in the Soudan in 1884, his first act was to telegraph to Mr. Rhodes, asking him to accompany him to Khartoum. Mr. Rhodes was then Treasurer of the Cape Colony, and so he was unable to accept General Gordon's invitation. Had it been otherwise, the recent history of Africa, both North and South, would have to be rewritten; for the life of one of these men and the death of the other are the two great factors which at this hour dominate the destinies of Africa.

If you want to understand Cecil Rhodes, it is necessary to begin by remembering that General Gordon knew him well and trusted him absolutely. General Gordon was the Bayard of our generation. No more absolutely selfless man ever served his country and his Queen. That pure and lofty spirit was never stained even by the calumny of those sordid souls who delight to impute to others the folly and baseness of their own nature. General Gordon was a man passionate for humanity, a very knight-errant of philanthropy, full of religious mysticism and an abiding sense of the reality and the power and the love of God. Alike in life and in death, he stands before the world a man of the stuff of which saints and martyrs are made; the most conspicuous and splendid type of the hero which Britain in these latter days has given to the world.

## A PARALLEL-

Both men were singularly selfless. Neither of them was married. Each of them had dedicated his life to the pursuit of a lofty ideal, over which both had brooded long years in the solitude of the African desert. To each of them, although in widely different ways, had come an abiding sense of the insignificance and brevity of life compared with the eternal realities which underlie the fleeting phenomena of this transitory life. It is difficult to say which despised more profoundly the gewgaws of pomp or the trappings of power, although Rhodes undoubtedly had a keener sense of the possibilities within the grasp of those who possess the sinews of war. Both were devoted to the service of their country, and each in his own way had a deep sense of the justice that was due to the dark-skinned races among whom their lot was cast.

Rhodes, like Gordon, was a man of action rather than a man of speech. Both possessed that rare gift of personal charm, which is due to a certain frank simplicity of manner and directness of speech. Both, in short, were real men and not shams, earnest men with a keen outlook into the world of men, strenuous to do with their might whatever their hand found to do in their brief working-day of life. Rhodes, like Gordon, was a man accustomed all his life to ponder the problems of empire. I said of him years ago that some men think in parishes, others in nations, but that Rhodes thinks in continents. So did Gordon. The voluminous papers which the latter wrote on questions of Imperial policy are a mine of political wisdom, in which statesmen might still delve and quarry with good profit.

## -AND A CONTRAST

There were differences between the two friends, as is natural between men one of whom believes in God Almighty, the Father of all men, as his Father and personal Lover of his soul; and the other to whom it seems but an even chance whether there be any God at all. One was a soldier; the other a diamond-digger. One had commanded armies and conducted negotiations in three continents. The other had merely made a million in South African finance. Nevertheless they knew and trusted each other; and in Gordon's confidence in Rhodes there is the best possible answer to the vulgar calumny which represents the great African as a mere millionaire of the Bourse, or an unscrupulous intriguer in Imperial politics.

## THE GREATNESS OF THE MAN

Cecil Rhodes is at this moment, notwithstanding his temporary eclipse after the unfortunate affair of the Jameson Raid, the greatest personage in the British Empire, bar two; the greatest man bar one. The Queen and the Queen's Prime Minister, Lord Salisbury, alone tower above the African Empire-builder in the estimation of the world, both within and without Greater Britain. After Mr. Rhodes, Mr. Chamberlain is a bad fourth. It was not until Mr. Rhodes fell on evil days, and was exposed to the bitter disappointments of unaccustomed failure and disasters, that the general public began to realize how great a man the Empire had reared in South Africa.

Mr. Rhodes was not a born millionaire. He was born, if not without a penny, at least in the usually impecunious condition of the younger son of a country parson. Neither did he start in life with any favourable handicap. He had to abandon his studies at Oxford in order to flee for his life to South Africa, to escape the fell disease which had apparently fastened itself upon his lungs. So ill was he before he left England, that his physicians never expected he would live for a twelve-month, even in South Africa. But the pure dry air of the African veldt worked wonders. Rhodes not only recovered his health, but being fortunate in the early days of diamond-digging in Kimberley, he laid the foundations of a great fortune. Then, with characteristic

doggedness and tenacity of purpose, he came home and completed his studies at Oxford. He was not a book-worm. His life at the University was more social than intellectual. But he went through the term of an undergraduate's study, graduated in due course, and returned to Africa. The episode is worth remembering, not merely because of the light it throws on Mr. Rhodes' character, but because it will be found hereafter to bear fruit in his aspirations after the realization of the unity of the English-speaking race.

## HOW HE MADE HIS FORTUNE

Young Rhodes was very fortunate in his financial operations. By degrees it became evident that he was coming to the top. The Jews there, as elsewhere, proved too many for the Gentiles. But there was one Gentile whom they could neither circumvent nor overcome. Ultimately, when the time came for the great amalgamation of all the various interest engaged in the diamond fields in one great trust or combine, Mr. Rhodes stood forth as the amalgamator, and the colossal De Beers Company is the monument of his success. He is reputed to be a rich man. It is true that he has the control of millions. But I seldom knew a rich man who had less ready cash. If any one were to give Mr. Rhodes a million sterling today, he would not have a penny of it tomorrow. As soon as he gets money, he spends it or invests it in the service of the Imperial idea.

## HIS RELATIONS TO THE NATIVES

In his dealings with his own workpeople, Mr. Rhodes is just and generous. It is the fashion to denounce his treatment of the Kaffirs, five thousand of whom earn a dollar a day in the diamond compound at Kimberley; but the Rev. Donald Macleod, one of the Queen's chaplains and editor of *Good Words*, who recently made a personal investigation of the facts of the case, has published a very remarkable testimony to the effect that after the missionaries no person has done so much for the African natives as Mr. Rhodes.

## HIS RELIGION

Mr. Rhodes' conception of his duties to his fellowmen rests upon a foundation as distinctly ethical and theistic as that of the old Puritans. If you could imagine an emperor of old Rome crossed with one of Cromwell's Ironsides, and the result brought up at the feet of Ignatius Loyola, you would have an amalgam not unlike that which men call Cecil Rhodes. But deep underlying all this there is the strong, earnest, religious conception of the Puritan. Mr. Rhodes is not, in the ordinary sense of the word, a religious man. He was born in a rectory, and, like many other clergymen's sons, he is no great Churchman. Upon many questions relating to the other world his one word is "I do not know." At present he has on his mind the development of Rhodesia, the laying of the telegraph line to Tanganyika, the Cape to Cairo railway, and the ultimate federation of South Africa. These four objects preoccupy him. So he went on digging for diamonds, and musing, as he digged, on the eternal verities, the truth which underlies all phenomena.

## HIS IDEAL

"What", asked Mr. Rhodes, "is the highest thing in the world? Is it not the idea of Justice? I know none higher. Justice between man and man—equal, absolute, impartial, fair play to all; that surely must be the first note of a perfected society. But, secondly, there must be Liberty, for without freedom there can be no justice. Slavery in any form which denies a man a right to be himself, and to use all his faculties to their best advantage, is, and must always be, unjust. And the third note of the ultimate towards which our race is bending must surely be that of Peace, of the industrial commonwealth as opposed to the military clan or fighting Empire." Anyhow, these three seem to Mr. Rhodes sufficient to furnish him with a metewand wherewith to measure the claims of the various races of the world to be regarded as the Divine instrument of future evolution. Justice, Liberty and Peace—these three. Which race in the world most promotes, over the widest possible area, a state of society having these three as corner-stones?

Who is to decide the question? Let all the races vote, and see what they will say. Each race will, no doubt, vote for itself, but who receives every second vote? Mr. Rhodes had no hesitation in arriving at the conclusion that the English race—the English-speaking man, whether British, American, Australian, or South African—is the type of the race which does now, and is likely to continue to do in the future, the most practical, effective work to establish justice, to promote liberty, and to ensure peace over the widest possible area of the planet.

# 8 CANADIAN CONTRIBUTION TO THE KHARTOUM RELIEF FORCE

*The Morning Chronicle, Quebec*
*September 16, 1884*

Report in the *Morning Chronicle* of remarks made by Governor-General Lord Lansdowne to the Canadian *voyageurs* destined for Egypt to form part of the Khartoum relief force.

... I am very glad to think that the Dominion is going to be represented on the expedition in which you are about to take part, your presence with it will show the whole world that the British Empire means something more than the British Islands and that in this part of it the Queen has loyal subjects who are ready to obey her summons and to serve under her flag.— (Loud applause.) It has been undertaken not for wanton aggression or selfish conquest but for one purpose and one only, the rescue of a man ["Chinese" Gordon] whose simplicity of character, whose personal courage and profound religious faith, qualities to which Canadians are not indifferent, have earned him the respect of the whole British Empire. (Applause.)

# 9 CANADIAN HERO HELPS KITCHENER RETAKE KHARTOUM

*The Province, Vancouver,*
*July 11, 1899*

Montreal will not be true to her traditions if she does not prepare a splendid reception for that gallant young Canadian Bimbashi Girouard, that "good man and true" as the Sirdar, Lord Kitchener, describes him. With the history of the fall of Mahdism the name of Girouard is firmly linked and Canadians of no matter what race may well take pride in the achievement of this young man by whose skill and energy the railroad was built across the desert almost as fast as the army could march. Being a son of Justice Girouard of the Supreme Court of Canada he has as good blood in his veins as there is in the Dominion and that another scion of an already distinguished house should bring it further honour will occasion no surprise. He has been a credit to the Royal Military College in particular but all Canada may well be proud of him. He is deserving of all the honour his native city can give him and a fitting welcome home should unquestionably be arranged.

# 10 THE CORONATION OF EDWARD VII: REFLECTIONS ON THE UNIVERSALITY OF THE BRITISH EMPIRE

*The Examiner, Peterborough*
*June 16, 1902*

The Coronation ceremonies will serve to bring into brilliant prominence the cosmopolitan character of the population of the Empire. This will be effected through the presence of military contingents composed of all races and coming from every clime and quarter of the Globe; for the crimson blazon of Imperial sovereignty reddens wide areas of the map of every continent, and of hundreds of the Isles of the sea. They will come from the furthest east and the furthest west ... And a significant feature is that Canada furnishes the highway of travel from the far east, to the heart of the empire, London. Two contingents composed of giant hillmen of India and the Chinese from Hong Kong ... are on their way to the coronation across Canada. These two contingents halted at Montreal where they were paraded on the Champs de Mars and inspected by Colonel Roy, D.O.C., in the presence of thronging thousands of the City of Montreal ... As these contingents, British in heart and allegiance but foreign in speech and aspect, stood on the historic square, the spectator who thought at all, could not help musing over the tremendous significance of the scene. As the statement of the Montreal *Star* tersely and comprehensively puts it: "There before him were British and Chinese troops, of Indian and Chinese birth, facing an inspecting officer of French Canadian origin on a parade ground made famous by French and British troops, in a city composed largely of British subjects of French descent, and in the Dominion of which a French Canadian is premier." This spectacle illustrates well the blending and welding spirit of British influence, under which divers nations and divers bloods are brought into unity of aim and harmony of purpose unparalleled on the face of the earth and unrecorded upon the page of any preceding history.

# 11 IMPERIALISM AS PART OF THE DIVINE PLAN

*The Orange Sentinel, Toronto*
*March 23, 1899*

... The public men of Canada can make up their minds as the public men of Britain have, that the movement towards Imperial Federation and subsequently to Anglo-Saxon Federation is beyond their power to control. It is part of the Divine plan for the civilization and regeneration of the world, and must come about, notwithstanding the puny efforts of puny men.

## 12  IMPERIALISM AND THE MISSIONARY IMPULSE: A CASE OF DISSIMILAR MOTIVATIONS?

*The Globe, Toronto*
*March 25, 1899*

Every age of Christian revival has been a missionary age. The quickened life immediately passes beyond itself. The thirst for empire, the indefinite enlargement of trade may be attributed to selfishness more or less enlightened, but the motive of missions is more or less unselfish. These journeyings, martyrdoms, voluntary surrender of self and all that the human heart holds dear for the sake of sharing with remote and unsympathetic peoples the Christian ideal and life, form the brightest and most reassuring chapter in the story of man.

## 13  IMPERIALISM AND PROTESTANTISM: A PARALLEL PROGRESS

*The Orange Sentinel, Toronto*
*July 27, 1899*

Eulogy by H. Hocken, P.M., L.O.L. 857 on twenty-five years of Protestant Progress.

That Protestantism has made wonderful progress during the past quarter of a century will be denied only by those who see in the statement of that fact a condemnation of their own religion. Statistics prove it, but more convincing than figures is the world-wide knowledge of the advancement made of the Protestant nations; as opposed to those that are distinctly Roman Catholic. The waste places of the earth are being reclaimed for Christianity by them; dark continents have been explored, and the light of Protestant doctrine carried to the benighted heathen; and oppression has been relieved and oppressors punished by those who represent the best ideals of Protestantism.

## 14  ROMAN CATHOLICS AND LOYALTY

*The Province, Victoria*
*January 23, 1897*

On 2 of this month (Jan.) a circular letter was sent out from Toronto, by persons unknown, to Protestant clergymen and leading citizens throughout Ontario. As a good deal of attention has been attracted to this particular document, it is here reproduced:

Patriotic Vigilance Committee

[Confidential]

Toronto, Ontario, Dec. 29, 1896

The gravity of the crisis brought upon the country by the result of the elections of June last, and the encouragement given to the disloyal elements of our population, has originated the formation of a Patriotic Vigilance Committee by a few citizens, determined to maintain by all means in their power the honour and integrity of the British flag and Dominion in Canada our country.

Acting in the dark, an insidious conspiracy has for several months been at work throughout the Dominion, aiming at the overthrow of the authority of our gracious Sovereign, the Queen and Empress, and the annexation of our beloved country to the United States. Behind what is ostensibly a political movement is plainly to be seen the hand of the Roman Catholic Church, the ever-watchful enemy of Protestant liberty. The movement is most active among the adherents of the Roman Catholic Church, and secret agents have been discovered propagating their disloyal and treasonable doctrines among them.

Although there are several members of the present Government who are known to be thoroughly and sincerely loyal, and one of them has given his entire approval to the issuing of this circular, the fact that the Government of Mr. Laurier owes its majority to the disloyal element, does not hold out the hope that they can successfully cope with the crisis in which we are.

We are therefore of the opinion that

steps should be taken forthwith to organize in every electoral district a Patriotic Vigilance Committee, to ascertain and record the views of all whom there is reasonable ground for suspecting of being in sympathy with the treasonable ideas that are already so widespread and to take such steps as may suggest themselves to check their further spread and manifestation. Also to inform the central Liberal-Conservative Associations and other loyal organizations of the country, of the names and character of such persons.

Every loyal citizen is invited to use his influence in his circle and neighbourhood to stamp out with vigour and determination, by every means in his power, all treason and disloyalty, by organizing or joining loyal associations, and to be prepared, if need be, to take up arms against the disloyal and all other conspirators against our Sovereign's authority, and so preserve the proud heritage bequeathed to us by our British forefathers.

> D.V.G.S.,
> Patriotic Vigilance Committee.
>
> God Save the Queen!

... plainly the work of some specially malignant Tupperites.

---

# 15 RACIAL DARWINISM AND IMPERIALISM

*The Canadian Churchman, Toronto*
*July 8, 1897*

Thoughts of Mrs. Clementina Fessenden of Hamilton on the development of a National Literature in Canada.

... A people's progress has its roots and is racy of their national institutions.

Our Canadian national institutions are no artificial fabric, devised by the wit of man, neither are they a new growth born here, but are a vast outspread of British institutions planted in the heyday of their manhood in this Canadian Dominion. Their germs were the primeval institutions of Britain's teutonic emigrants, nurtured thirteen centuries ago in that great national institution the Christian Church; their flag with its cross still bears the token of their birth.

... Its history broadening down from precedent to precedent, has been the pure development of the free institutions of our Teutonic forefathers...

As the close of the organic evolution of the body makes for human life a beginning for that mental evolution which strengthens and beautifies that life in its body, so there is before us an analogous development of our national life, British North American Acts and Imperial Federalism ever increasing the efficiency of our institutions and adapting them to the ever new conditions and exigencies, world-wide as are its world, embracing new homes. This, then, is our Canadian life, with which our Canadian literature must keep step and be its tongue.

---

# 16 CANADA'S DUTY TO THE EMPIRE

*The Manitoba Free Press, Winnipeg*
*January 6, 1896*

The Anglo-American dispute over the Venezuelan Boundary elicits a definition of Canada's duty to the Empire.

Canadians complained and with reason of the bitter tone of the American people breathing violent and unnatural hatred of Great Britain, as their response to President Cleveland's Venezuelan message. It was as venomous as it was sudden and surprising—surprising because the two nations had for years been drawing more closely together...

But if we were surprised and shocked at this, we have to acknowledge the frankness with which American newspapers express their admiration for the loyalty and devotion of the Canadian people which the event has occasioned. Some of them regard our manifestation of attachment to the Mother country as a thing to be wondered at, but all admit that it is genuine and very much to our credit. Indeed it has been the occasion of many pleasant and flattering things that have been said of us. We are naturally gratified at these expressions but they are remarkable chiefly as showing that the United States has grown great enough to be generous, although it cannot yet always be just...

... The lot of Canadians is a happy one. To other people other skies may be dearer, but we love our own. We love the rugged hills not less than the quiet meadows of our country; we love its prairies, its rivers, its lakes, and even its rocks. We love it all the more because the great red cross of St. George waves over it, assuring us that we are part and parcel of the greatest empire the world has ever seen. Our loyalty to the old flag is a thing that among Canadians is understood as well as felt, and should trouble come between the mother country and the United States, which God forbid, we shall be found in the thick of it, perhaps not mighty, but doing the best of brave, earnest men fighting for home and motherland.

---

# 17 IMPERIALISM AND CANADIAN-AMERICAN RELATIONS

*The Globe, Toronto*
*December 6, 1897*

Speech by Hon. George Ross,
Minister of Education for Ontario.

### The Question of Reciprocity

Next in importance to preferential trade with Great Britain is the subject of a reciprocity treaty between Canada and the United States. In dealing with this question one is embarrassed by the twofold interest which seems to be involved in it— the interest of the mother country and the interest of Canada. In the mother country the opinion very generally prevails that the unfriendly commercial relations existing between Canada and the United States are a menace to the peace of the empire. It has been the ambition of English states-

men for the last fifty years to remove this supposed irritation by treaties and concessions, many of which were none too favorable to Canada. The first attempt of this kind was the Ashburton treaty of 1846, by which it is universally admitted Canada was greatly the loser territorially on her eastern as well as on her western frontier. The Washington treaty of 1871 was less disastrous, although it involved concessions in the inland waters and canals of Canada for which no equivalent was granted in the inland waters of the United States. It is within the memory of most of us also how the damages to Canada, by the Fenian invasion of 1866 were entirely overlooked by the Geneva award with respect to the Alabama claims. If past experience is any guide in dealing with the removal of this so-called irritation, there is but little hope for its permanent removal by any reciprocity treaty to which Canada could assent.

But there is another side to the question. While Canada has already made many sacrifices, far too great in my opinion for any advantage that has been conferred upon her. It is well to point out that she is in no sense responsible for the irritation which is the alleged cause of our unhappy international relations. Our first serious quarrel with the United States took place in 1812. To this quarrel Canada was in no way a party, although she was the greatest sufferer. The irritation arising out of this war affected our relations with the adjoining republic for many years. We did not forget, and we could not forget in a day the wanton invasion of our soil by American armies, and the destruction of our cities and towns by the gunboats and the torches of the invaders.

Again, in 1866, we were called upon to repel the Fenian hordes which crossed the border to plunder and destroy our country without any provocation on our part. That invasion, no doubt, caused much irritation, and very properly so, but from no fault of ours. We took no part in fomenting the rebellion in the southern States; we were not friendly to the slave-holder or his traffic in human flesh. On the contrary, we afforded the slave an asylum from his persecutors, and 33,000 of our sons enlisted in the army of the north to maintain the unity and perpetuity of the republic. We have not forgotten this wanton invasion of our soil: for the irritation which it produced the blame is not with us: the blame is with the United States and the authorities who winked at the well-known intention of the invaders.

## Commercial Attacks Upon Canada

In recent years the attack upon Canada was not of a military but of a commercial character, and was all the more insidious because disguised under the form of tariffs and duties, alleged to be necessary for the maintenance of the revenues of the republic. The repeal of the reciprocity treaty of 1854, immediately after the close of the American war, was evidently an attack upon the commerce of this country, and all apologies to the contrary notwithstanding, the same remark will hold true of the majority of the tariff bills that have been submitted to Congress since that date. The remarks made during the discussions, notably on the McKinley bill, clearly indicated that the intention of American statesmen in taxing our barley, our coal and our lumber, as well as other products of the country, was to cripple the trade of Canada as much as possible. Still more significant are the alien labor laws and the invidious provisions of the Dingley bill with respect to the products of our Canadian forests. Is it not evident, therefore, to the most superficial observer that no concession on the part of Great Britain to the United States—not even the payment of claims under the Geneva award, well-known to be greatly in excess of the damages inflicted—has had the desired effect of developing a spirit of international friendship such as we should naturally expect ought to exist between two countries of the same blood and speaking the same language? The conclusion is thus irresistibly forced upon us that, so far as Canada is concerned, it is utterly useless to entertain the idea of a reciprocity treaty with the United States for the purpose of removing either present or future irritation. Our experience, in many cases bitter and humiliating, is against any expectation of that kind. I am therefore, reluctantly I must admit, obliged to eliminate from the consideration of this question all speculation with regard to its effect upon international relations.

## Commercial Aspects of Reciprocity

But, it will be said, even if reciprocity with the United States does not promote more friendly relations with the American Republic it may nevertheless be a source of profit commercially to the people of Canada. In proof of this proposition the treaty effected by Lord Elgin in 1854 is constantly cited. It is not for me to dispute the opinion of commercial authorities respecting the treaty of 1854. I would merely in passing point out that during the last five years of that treaty the conditions of trade in the United States were exceptional. The republic was involved in a civil war, the most gigantic of modern times. Over 1,000,000 men were withdrawn from the productive industries of the country. They had to be fed and clothed at all hazards, and for several years Canada was literally drawn upon for the supplies required by the American army as well as to make up the diminution in other departments of trade and commerce caused by the withdrawal of so many men from their usual avocations. Had the treaty of 1854 been continued for some years longer it is doubtful whether the advantages to Canada, great as they no doubt were, would not have abated substantially by the resuscitation of industries which the civil war had destroyed.

But it will be said again, even admitting your argument with regard to the treaty of 1854, there is still room for the interchange of products which would be of mutual advantage to the two countries. Using the word advantage in a strictly commercial sense, that statement is possibly true: for instance, I think reciprocity in coal and lumber, and perhaps in a few other articles, would be a benefit to both Canada and the United States. It would be folly to say that nations as well as individuals could not profitably exchange products. Laws of exchange all the world over are against any such assumption; but valuable as the exchange of commodities may be to the development of a country when such exchange becomes a subject of treaty, questions of an international character arise which must not be lost sight of. Trade then becomes a political as well as a commercial question, and it is to its political aspect that I wish to call your attention.

## Dangers of Reciprocity

(1) A reciprocity treaty may be used as an admission that the weaker nation making such a treaty is dependent upon the stronger nation for a market, or such a treaty may foster a feeling of dependence in the weaker nation upon the markets of the stronger nation. In either case any such feeling would be prejudicial to Canada. Though weaker numerically than the United States, we must resist resolutely everything that would propagate a feeling of dependence upon her either for our commerce or our national existence. Such a feeling would utterly mar the true spirit of Canadian nationality.

(2) The repeal of a reciprocity treaty by which new channels of trade were opened up might be held by a stronger nation *in terrorem* [sic] over the weaker, as destructive to the trade so established and as a means of wresting concessions inimical to the prosperity of the weaker nation. Nay, more, the consequence of such repeal might be made suggestive of political union as the only way of averting the commercial disasters which such repeal involved.

(3) Having invested, as I have already pointed out, nearly $1,000,000,000 of money for the transportation of our goods to the seaboard, would we not be doing an injustice to the Canadian and British capital so invested if we diverted the transportation of our goods to American railways and canals? A similar observation would apply to the capital and labor employed in transportation. A nation that cannot give employment to its own people very soon becomes depopulated.

(4) At best any market based upon a treaty is a temporary one. On what commercial principle can we justify any effort to set up a temporary market where a permanent one is within reach and where we have already agreed to pay large subsidies and have undertaken permanent charges for the purpose of reaching it? For all time to come Great Britain will be dependent on the outside world for her food products. The United States can more than supply her own people. Everything points to the market of Great Britain as the only permanent market for the people of Canada. (5) Trade follows the flag and British subjects follow British trade. For the further settlement of this country as well as for strengthening our relations with the empire our obvious policy is to develop trade with Great Britain.

## There Should be No Haste

For these reasons there should be no haste in the efforts to negotiate a reciprocity treaty with the United States. We owe it to ourselves that we should not approach the Americans in any spirit of dependence or subserviency. It should be distinctly understood that we ask no favors in the American market for which we are unable to give an ample equivalent in the Canadian market, and no condition involving the sacrifice of any vested right or any consideration whatsoever as to the use of our waterways, our railroads or our fisheries should be put in the scale as a counterpoise to any privilege afforded us in the markets of the United States. A commercial treaty that cannot be made on a commercial basis pure and simple should not be made at all. On this point there should be neither parleying nor pandering. If we cannot pay in kind for what we get we must not take the risk of supplementing the transaction by any other consideration.

In conclusion I desire to say that while it is the object of the British Empire League to promote the unity of the empire, if I understand its principles aright, it is equally solicitous in promoting the peace of the empire. In fact no better guarantee can be given for the peace of the world than the strengthening of the moral and commercial power of Great Britain and her colonies. Her army and her navy may suggest the terrible consequences to the nation which provokes her to a contest either by land or by sea, and powerful as that army and navy may be, her enemies might have the temerity to believe it could be successfully overcome, were it not for the reflection that her subjects in every zone constitute a grand reserve, if need be, for any national emergency.

> "for the sire lives in his sons,
> And they pay their father's debt—
> And the lion has left a whelp
> Wherever his claw was set."

---

# 18  IMPERIAL UNITY FOR THE DEFENCE OF CANADA

*The Globe, Toronto*
*April 7, 1899*

A Speech by Colonel Denison

There is one point I wish to press upon this meeting; there has been in the last 25 or 30 years a revolution in the affairs of the world in reference to national relations and methods of defence. The policy seems to have imperceptibly grown up of uniting for mutual protection and defence. Germany has united, and we remember that it was accomplished under the stress and trial of war ... Italy as a result of three wars has been united and consolidated. The United States during the last year have launched out into the politics of the world, have adopted expansion as their policy, and are pressing their views on the Filipinos with rifles, maxims, and field guns. We have discovered this year once more by hard facts what history in all ages has shown— that nations cannot expect to exist upon the security of their natural moral rights, unless those rights are supported by physical strength. Spain has been taught that might prevails and she has been crushed and humiliated, for doing what the United States are now obliged to do themselves in the Philippine Islands. The greatest lesson of all, however, which this last year has taught us is that which we learn from the impending fate of China. There is a nation of three hundred to four hundred millions of people, honest traders, I am told, cer-tainly most inoffensive and unaggressive; a nation which from its peaceful character, industrious habits and natural reserve, should have been the last to have aroused hostility. It has neglected its defences ... nations can only enjoy their freedom by being able to defend it, and that the true policy for nations under present conditions is to be closely united within themselves, to be thoroughly organized and equipped ...

If we Canadians desire to be free and safe, it must be in that Empire to which we are attached by every tie and to which we must be ready to give our strength for the common defence, if we expect the enor-mous reserve force of that empire to be at our back if our life as a free people should ever be threatened. It is necessary, there-fore, for the prosperity and safety of all the parts, that the United Kingdom, India, Australasia, South Africa, and Canada should all be firmly united so as to show a square front to any enemies that might attack us.

---

# 19  CANADIAN SELF-CONFIDENCE: SOLIDARITY WITH THE EMPIRE

*The London Advertiser*
*September 20, 1900*

The following is a speech of
Hon. George W. Ross, Premier of Ontario
and Vice-President of the Toronto branch of
the British Empire League, which was reprinted
by the *London Advertiser.*

Narrowness has been the bane of Canada for half a century. Canada had first shivered at every sight of the United States flag and believed that we would be ab-sorbed by the Republic; then we thought that we had a right to exist on our half of the continent, then we decided that we had clear title to more than half a continent, and now we find a substantial interest in the whole empire. Pessimism has spent it-self in politics; the day of the pigmy is gone by. The watchword now is: Canada, one and inseparable, now and forever, an in-tegral part of the empire. Let us bear our burdens of the empire like honourable men, and whenever Britain goes forth to battle, Canada's sons and daughters in their field of duty, will be found standing by the honour of Old England.

## 20 CANADA'S IMPERIAL RESPONSIBILITIES

*The Globe, Toronto*
*November 26, 1900*

... It is of course always easier to rejoice in the possession of power than to ponder over its responsibilities but it is only by the more difficult process that progress can be made in the right direction. ... He (George Parkin) gives a warning against the jingo spirit. "We should seek to justify our tremendous place in the world by the absolute justice of our rule, by the fairness and consideration with which we treated other people, by the repression of the aggressive Anglo-Saxon spirit and by giving great and convincing proofs of the correctness of Lord Roseberry's statement that the British Empire was the greatest secular agency for good that existed in the world."

... The central truth is that our destiny depends on ourselves; that we must rise by our own efforts, and that if calamities overtake us they are more likely to be due to our own faults and weaknesses than to the wicked designs of other people.

To go back to Dr. Parkin's theme. What is the Imperial duty and responsibility of the Canadian people? In the last analysis it will be found that it is almost identical with their national duty. There is nothing narrow or selfish in this view. It simply recognizes that there is a division of labour in the empire, as in everything else. In the nature of things, however much we may be interested in other parts of the empire ... we can take very little share in their government and development. Some have free Parliaments like our own; some are governed in a paternal way by a trained civil service organized in England. If any of them were threatened by a foreign enemy, by famine or pestilence, we should doubtless go to their aid ...

So it should not be forgotten that one of the greatest services which Canada renders to the Empire is to keep Great Britain free from all anxiety, so far as this part of the world is concerned. We have our problems of expansion but they are peaceful ones ... It is certain that the more our wheat lands are settled, the more our supplies of coal, iron, nickel, etc. are developed the more we shall add to the strength of the Empire, as well as of Canada ... The Empire is strong when its parts are strong.

## 21 MORAL INFLUENCE OF CANADA ON THE EMPIRE

*The Star, Montreal*
*January 22, 1900*

In so far as the colonies can strengthen the tendency towards righteousness in Britain's foreign policy, they will be doing a great service to the world and a greater one to the Empire. No power that does not deserve to live will in the long run survive; and when Britain begins to found her empire upon power, unjustified by liberty and justice, she will find herself building upon sand.

## 22 CANADIAN NATIONALISM AND IMPERIALISM

*The London Advertiser*
*September 28, 1900*

Report of a speech by Premier Ross.

There is no antagonism in my opinion between Canadianism and imperialism. The one is but the expansion of the other. To be a true Canadian, under existing conditions, is to place yourself in harmony with the spirit of the empire, with its love of liberty, with its resolute defence of its rights, with its enterprise, with its disposition to deal even-handed justice to its subjects, irrespective of race and creed, with its interest in all that refines and ennobles the human race and with its unfailing trust in the principles of our common Christianity. That is imperialism as I understand it. That is Canadianism as I would like it to be, if we are all true to the traditions and the spirit of the empire to which we belong. It is in that spirit that we will best overcome the petty jealousies of a new country and attain that rank and dignity for which nature and providence have, in my opinion, amply prepared us.

---

## 23 CANADA REJECTS IMPERIAL FEDERATION

*The Province, Victoria*
*March 20, 1897*

Imperial Federation for Great Britain would bring with it an increase in the difficulties of her position which would only serve to augment her "splendid isolation." She could look for no effective assistance from the colonies. They for their part would reluctantly consent to send a part, and a small part at that, of their revenues to London as a contribution to the defence of the Empire.

To the British Empire as a whole federation would probably be but the prelude to dislocation. The establishment of the machinery of Government common to both Mother Country and colonies would always involve a certain danger. Such an arrangement would always be attended with all the greater difficulty because, in the general council which would preside over the destinies of the Empire the Home Country, of which the population is by far the greatest, would always have a preponderating influence. It must not be forgotten that it was the unjust imposition of taxes which brought about the American Revolution. It is true that the Americans were not represented in the British Parliament, whereas the Colonists would be in the Federal Council. But they would not have the majority, and it would not be long before discontents discovered that such representation was illusory. "A slender thread" said Mr. Chamberlain a year ago, "binds her colonies to Britain; but I recollect having visited factories where through a delicate wire there passed an electrical current capable of working the most powerful machines." No doubt; but there are limits to the strength of the wire. If too great a force is transmitted the wire burns out. Perhaps a rupture would ensue were the cords which bind the mother country and her children too tightly pulled, and it may very well be that the present state of relationship which has tended to the Empire's development is best calculated to promote its duration.

---

## SIR JOHN'S RIGHTFUL SUCCESSOR.

SPIRIT OF SIR JOHN—My old party may have my effigy with them in this campaign, but the record and influence of my life as a statesman is with you, Sir Wilfrid.

*[Reproduced from J. W. Bengough: Cartoons of the Campaign 1900, Toronto: The Poole Publishing Company, 1900.]*

## 24 AN ENGLISH CANADIAN DISSENTING VOICE: IMPERIALISM AND SOCIAL JUSTICE

*The Province, Victoria*
*March 6, 1897*

An appeal has been made throughout the Empire for the relief of our fellow subjects in India ... To what end? Simply and solely that the same old evil may be perpetuated *ad infinitum*. The Bourbon motto might well be adopted by our Indian Administration, for truly in the matter of recurring famine it is the case of *Rien appris, rien oublié*. The average individual puts his hand in his pocket for the fifth or fifteenth time, as the case may be, and plonks down his five dollar bill, with the comforting sensation of a duty that is done ... It was recently pointed out in these columns that poverty is not a God-given gift to man; that it comes under the heading of a preventable disease. Famine, whether in India or elsewhere, is but a form of poverty, and may therefore be put in the same category. There is no element of the Divine in any form of poverty, and its origin can be traced in that aphorism of Burns:

Man's inhumanity to man makes countless thousands mourn.

[Eighteen million have died even though India exports food]; the expenses of government have been enormously increased under Imperial rule; thus the relentless taxation of a people so miserably poor that the masses are not more than half fed, is robbing them of their scanty means of cultivating the soil [and forcing them to borrow at high interest rates for vast public works]. In one of the famines of Southern India it is estimated that 6 million people died of starvation, yet the taxes were not remitted; and the salt tax, already prohibitory to the great bulk of these poverty-stricken people, was increased forty per cent. Could the cultivators of the soil retain their little capital and be released from the drain, which reduces them in non-famine years to the borderland of starvation, reviving industry, assuming more productive forms, would enable them to make provision against days of drought and scarcity. The real cause of want in India, as it is the real cause of want everywhere else in the world, is the rapacity of man, not the niggardliness of nature.

... What is true of India is equally true of Ireland. Nothing is better calculated to make the blood boil than the cold and callous accounts of the grinding tyranny to which the Irish people have been subjected, and to which, and not to any inability of the soil to support population, Irish pauperism and Irish famine are to be attributed. How could there fail to be pauperism and famine in a country where rack-rents wrested from the cultivator of the soil all the produce of the soil except just enough to maintain life in good seasons; where tenure at will forbade improvements; where the tenant dared not accumulate capital for fear it should be demanded in rent; where absentee landlords drained away, without return, at least a fourth of the produce of the soil?

## 25 A FRENCH CANADIAN DISSENTING VOICE: IMPERIALISM MEANS BLOODSHED AND TAXATION

*L'Interprète, Montebello, Quebec*
*October 12, 1893*

The young Henri Bourassa gives his view of the importance of the British Empire for Canada. Note that this is before any questions of military imperialism had been raised in Canada.

Grind the people down with taxes, bleed them white for the maintenance of the British Empire, and in compensation England will from time to time choose some good Tory and send him here and there to conclude treaties in which Canadian interests will generally be sacrificed to the interests of England. The people cry famine; It does not matter, Toryism is satisfied, the Empire is united, Britannia rules.[1]

[1]quoted from M. P. O'Connell, "The Ideas of Henri Bourassa," *Canadian Journal of Economics and Political Science*, XIX, 3 (August, 1953), p. 364.

## Section II

Unity For Trade: The Imperial Preferences, 1896-1902

# 1 HISTORY OF THE IDEA OF IMPERIAL PREFERENCE

*The Globe, Toronto*
*August 18, 1897*

A chapter of Mr. Pope's life of Sir John Macdonald is devoted to Imperial Federation. Sir John did not believe that a Parliamentary federation of the empire was practicable or that a uniform tariff could be established throughout the empire, but he saw no insuperable difficulty in the way of a commercial union between Britain and the colonies, his idea being a mutually preferential commercial arrangement between England and Canada, under which a small duty should be levied upon foreign corn coming into Britain, and a similar advantage afforded to British manufactures by Canada.

After the general elections of 1891, Sir John received a letter from W. H. Smith, then leader of the British House of Commons, congratulating him and speaking of the McKinley tariff. What can we do? ... Sir John replied that if the Conservatives won the British elections some Imperial policy could be framed and carried out. Meanwhile manufacturers and their working people should be taught that they can find friendly and expanding markets in the colonies if they are treated in the same spirit. He then suggested that Canada would be ready to give a preference of 5 or even 10 per cent to the British goods if our products received a corresponding preference in England. It is probable that Sir John meant a preference of 5 or 10 per cent to British goods, not of the duty.

In the session of 1891, after Sir John's death, both Houses of Parliament adopted an address to the Queen, asking for the withdrawal of Britain from the German and Belgian Treaties in order that an obstacle to preferential trade might be removed. In 1892 Mr. McNeill, a Conservative MP, who afterwards broke with the Government on the Manitoba School question moved a resolution declaring that Canada would be willing to give a preference to British goods if and when Canada received similar treatment in the British market.

The result of the votes of 1891 and 1892 showed that Parliament was unanimous in the desire to give preferential treatment to Britain, but was divided as to the means. It is fair to give the credit to the Conservatives in the House for taking the initiative. It is fair to give the Liberals the credit for finding out the means of carrying out the wish of Parliament.

The fatal defect in the Conservative plan was that it was conditional and that the condition relegated preferential treatment of Canada to the distant future. Canada was to act only in the event of Britain revolutionizing her fiscal system. It was left to a Liberal, Mr. Davies, to make the suggestion which culminated in the notable achievements of the present year. In effect he said: Let us offer Britain not a bargain but a free gift, and leave the rest to herself. We are a part of the British Empire; our goods are freely admitted into British ports; let us freely, voluntarily and immediately reduce the duty on goods mainly imported from Great Britain. The House being Conservative preferred Mr. McNeill's plan. Nothing substantial came of it and the obstacle presented by the German and Belgian Treaties remained until a few weeks ago.

# 2 THE CONSERVATIVE PARTY SUPPORTS THE IDEA

*The Citizen, Ottawa*
*May 6, 1896*

In the election campaign of 1896 the Conservatives stressed imperial preferential tariffs as a means of developing Canadian trade and strengthening imperial unity. The following extract is from a speech of Sir Charles Tupper.

At the Colonial Conference which met at Ottawa in 1894, a series of resolutions were adopted in favour of closer trade relations within the Empire, involving the principle of preferential trade arrangements. This opens a hopeful view to Canada. During the past few years, our export trade with Great Britain has undergone great expansion, and particularly the products of the farm. Our total trade with that country has increased from $67,288,848 in 1879 to an average of $101,011,304 during that past five years; while the annual increase of farm products alone has increased from $32,028,611 to $50,106,898 in the same period. With a tariff based upon mutual concession, it is reasonable to expect a still greater development of our trade in that market and we should, at the same time, be rendering material assistance towards the unity and strengthening of the empire—without involving a lessening of the protection to our industries. On patriotic and commercial grounds, therefore, this measure is worthy of your cordial support.

## 3  THE LIBERAL PARTY SUPPORTS PREFERENTIAL TRADE

*The Globe, Toronto*
*May 20, 1896*

The question of preferential trade between the colonies and the British Isles is receiving a wide measure of attention throughout the Dominion, interest being intensified by the agricultural depression at present resulting from artificial restraints and economic changes. The disposal of the surplus food supply is the most important commercial question now before the Canadian people, and as the development of the west goes forward under the stimulus of better political auspices the surplus products for export must rapidly increase. Evidently a preferential tariff in the British Isles giving favourable treatment to this growing surplus would be of great advantage not only to our farming interests but to the Dominion at large. Canada is apprehensive of Russian, Argentine, and other foreign competition in the British market... With a preferential tariff in Britain placing us and other colonies in an exceptionally favourable position the disappointing slowness of this development would at once give place to a forward

movement such as the Dominion has often hoped for but never experienced.

## 4  THE FLOW OF BRITISH CAPITAL INTO CANADA

*The Star, Montreal*
*July 6, 1896*

Not a little talk is being heard just now of the probable investment of British capital in Canada. Mr. E. B. Osler, a newly elected member for West Toronto, brought home from the London Chambers of Commerce Congress, news of an abundance of "home" capital ready to flow into the country. Now a British capitalist who has been looking into the Rainy River district tells a Toronto reporter that there is "any amount of money in Britain" waiting for investment, and he thinks that Canada is "a more favourable place to invest than the United States" because of this silver agitation, which has unsettled affairs.

... However this may be, the spectacle of a great party (the Democrats) campaigning vigorously for what is equivalent to a reduction in the value of the dollar, and consequently a reduction of the value of every debt expressed in dollars cannot be reassuring to Englishmen who have loaned money in the United States. More than that, the readiness of a large section of the people to unsettle the financial basis of the nation must disquiet would-be investors and incline them to look for an outlet in a community whose financial principles are fixed and safe. The Canadian banking and financial systems are models in the way of security and firmness; and British capital cannot do better than follow the flag on this continent.

## 5  THE ADVANTAGE OF FREE TRADE

*The Morning Chronicle, Halifax*
*January 16, 1897*

New South Wales is the Free Trade Colony of Australia. In keeping with her free trade policy she is the most progressive and prosperous of all the Australian colonies. It will therefore not be matter for surprise to learn that she leads them all in ocean shipping. ... These figures are exceedingly suggestive of the advantages which a free trade policy gives a country in the matter of shipping and foreign trade. The people of Canada should not miss this point.

# 6 LAURIER'S TRADE MISSION TO WASHINGTON, 1897

*The Citizen, Ottawa*
*February 10, 1897*

Our representatives in Washington are not getting much encouragement, and to say the truth they deserve little. They have gone on a begging mission to Washington without being asked and without being encouraged, and their attitude in the presence of the American politicians has been neither dignified nor patriotic. Here we are an integral portion of the British empire, and yet our cabinet ministers represent themselves as more favourable to the extension of trade relations with the United States than with the mother land.

... It is clear that the party in power has not yet got rid of its pro-American and anti-British taint. Although we owe Britain everything that one country can owe another, and although we have received from the United States nothing but unfriendly treatment, still we are seeking at Washington to advance the latter at the expense of the former. Leaving out of the question the fact that our allegiance is to the British Crown, the attitude of our negotiators is undignified, humiliating and ungrateful.

# 7 THE LIBERALS, THE BUDGET AND THE COMING TARIFF

*The Star, Montreal*
*April 21, 1897*

Tomorrow will be budget day ... Liberals are now much more practical—in the campaign of 1896 the city spokesmen had put much emphasis on protection—so the Liberal Tariff will not endanger the industrial system of the country.

Meanwhile the rising spirit of Imperialism has been gaining force, and in this year of the Diamond Jubilee has risen to a greater vigor than ever. The possibility of fostering trade within the Empire by adjusting our tariffs to that end, has passed beyond the "fad" stage. ... Leading statesmen in the United Kingdom talk hopefully of the prospect of bringing the Empire to a state of development in which it can feed itself; and the leading colonial press all round the world are discussing eagerly the possibility of discriminating in favour of British goods. The strengthening of this sentiment, coinciding with the attainment of power by the Liberals, appears to bring with it a solution for the political problem that confronts them. They are pledged to reduce the tariff, they are pledged not to let in a destructive flood of competition among our industries, and the renewed hostility of the American tariff policy forbids any lowering of the wall on that side. What then can they do except reduce the tariff on the British side? And this is precisely the course that the mounting imperialist spirit points out to them ...

# 8 THE NEW TARIFF

*The Globe, Toronto*
*April 26, 1897*

On April 22, 1897 Laurier's Minister of Finance introduced a budget extending preferential tariffs to Great Britain.

By the new tariff Canada claims the supreme right of self-government, asserts her authority as one of the dominating forces of the new continent, and declares her full citizenship in a world-spreading empire. We have, however, the argument that under Imperial treaties Canada may not discriminate in favour of the empire to which she belongs ... This would mean that on the vital questions of trade and of revenue we are not self-governing and that we hold our imperial citizenship under restrictions and limitations that hamper us in our dealings with foreign countries, and hamper us equally in the field of domestic concerns. This, too, while we as British citizens have no voice in the negotiation of the treaties which restrict our liberties and limit our right of self-government. This would indeed be a diluted colonialism, a very badge and stigma of inferiority for British citizens who do not happen to live in the home kingdoms. But it seems to us very certain that the British authorities will not seek to affix this stigma of inferiority upon the Canadian people ... The Liberals of Canada are not seeking to discriminate against England, they are not seeking to escape Imperial responsibilities, they do not want to pull down the empire ... We have struck the first blow for a real, practical Imperial federation while we make no special discrimination against any other country, and it does not seem to us that Great Britain, under threat and suspicion from the four corners of the earth, should bless the work and give God-speed to the Liberal Government of Canada ... But in this event a fatal blow would be dealt to preferential trading arrangements within the empire, and the agencies that are making for Imperial union on the basis of inter-imperial trade would have received notice to withdraw from the field.

# 9  THE NEW TARIFF: A MARITIME VIEW

*The Morning Chronicle, Halifax*
*April 23, 1897*

The first substantive step in tariff reform was taken in the tariff which was brought down in the House of Commons yesterday.

The Government are keeping faith with the people in materially lightening the burdens resting upon them and their industries, and in lessening the restrictions imposed on trade by the national policy. They are keeping faith with the business and manufacturing interests of the country by guarding against drastic reductions of duty which would unduly disturb business or too severely press upon industries which have grown up in the artificial atmosphere created by the national policy ... The principle advocated by the Liberals—that of reducing the duties on goods imported chiefly from Britain—has been carried out; in fact Canada gives Great Britain preferential treatment—a course which will be heartily approved by the people of this country ... And now that we have taken the first substantial step on the tariff reform road, it will be comparatively easy to take additional steps in the future in the direction of a substantial measure to free trade.

# 10  CONSERVATIVE SUPPORT FOR THE NEW TARIFF

*The Star, Montreal*
*April 23, 1897*

The general feeling in Canada with regard to the new tariff will be one of profound satisfaction ... courageous enactment of preferential trade with Britain—for that is what we understand the minimum duty clause to mean.

# 11  LIBERAL TARIFF ERASES TORY DISCRIMINATION

*The Globe, Toronto*
*April 23, 1897*

The feature of the new tariff bill that will in many quarters at least, be most heartily commended is that which at last sets right a state of affairs of which Liberal speakers and Liberal newspapers have complained for years past. This was the practical discrimination under the Tory tariff against British goods. For example, the average duty on importations from Britain in 1896 was 22 per cent, while the average duty on goods from the United States was 13 per cent. The percentage varied in different years but it was always markedly against the mother country ... It stamped our customs laws with the stigma of ingratitude ...

## 12 COMPLIMENTS FROM LONDON

*The Times, London*
*April 26, 1897*
[*in The Globe, Toronto, April 27, 1897*]

The satisfaction of Canadians over the compliments the new tariff policy received in London is reflected in the reporting of the statements of *The Times* of London in the front leader of the *Globe*, Toronto, April 27, 1897.

The new departure is most gratifying to all who desire to see the empire knitted more closely together. It is the most remarkable step yet made towards the fiscal federation of the empire.

... If other British colonies follow suit and the day comes that free trade exists from one frontier of the empire to the other, it will be mutual satisfaction to recall the circumstances of the first step in the initiation of that policy.

## 13 LAURIER IS MORE ENGLISH THAN CANADIAN

*Le Monde, Montreal*
*April 26, 1897* [translation]

The tariff will bring about a commercial crisis. Several business men are closing their factories.

The tariff continues to be the main topic of conversation and a steadily increasing number of people are finding it both im-practical and unsound. People are saying that Mr Laurier has particularly applied himself on Britain's behalf without bothering about the interests of this country, just as if he were a British instead of a Canadian minister.

## 14 THE NEW TARIFF: VARIATION ON AN OLD THEME

*The Daily Sun, Saint John*
*April 26, 1897*

The most interesting feature in the Fielding tariff is the preferential platform. In adopting this in respect to the British Empire, he has taken over, though with a most serious omission, the policy of Mr. Foster and the liberal-conservative party. This imperial preference also is a policy which has been denounced and derided by the liberal party. It is opposed to the doctrine that we must legislate chiefly for the continent "to which we belong." If it did not include other European countries as well as Great Britain it would be a recognition of the fact that we belong to the empire rather than to the continent. It would be an endorsation, in its professed principles, of the policy platform of the British Empire League and of the old Imperial Federation League. Those of us who for years have been advocating a policy of preference to the mother country, and to the British colonies, have now our day of triumph in the pretences if not the performances of the old commercial unionists. If the thing done were what it professed to be, it would not be in the least disturbing that it comes in the way of a complete and unqualified surrender on the part of the party and the men who have made the imperialists the butt of their ridicule and scorn.

It remains to be seen whether the government will be able to carry their preferential scheme into effect ... At all events the government has, so far as trade with the empire is concerned, the good wishes of loyal Canadians. The ministers may have gone wrong, but he is a poor liberal-conservative who will not hope that yet good may come of it.

---

# 15 RUDYARD KIPLING SALUTES CANADA

*The Star, Montreal*
*April 28, 1897*

Rudyard Kipling wrote his poem "Our Lady of the Snows" as a tribute to Canada and her pro-empire tariff policy. Here are three of the six stanzas that originally appeared in *The Times* of London, April 27, 1897, and were reprinted widely in the Canadian press.

Our Lady of the Snows

A Nation spoke to a Nation,
A Queen sent word to a Throne:
"Daughter am I in my mother's house,
But mistress in my own.
The gates are mine to open,
As the gates are mine to close,
And I set my house in order,"
Said our Lady of the Snows.

"My speech is clean and single,
I talk of common things—
Words of the wharf and the market-place
And the ware the merchant brings:
Favour to those I favour,
But a stumbling-block to my foes.
Many there be that hate us,"
Said our Lady of the Snows.

"Carry the word to my sisters—
To the Queens of the East and the South.
I have proven faith in the Heritage
By more than the word of the mouth.
They that are wise may follow
Ere the world's war-trumpet blows,
But I—I am first in the battle,"
Said our Lady of the Snows.

Rudyard Kipling, 1897.

---

# 16 LAURIER: TOOL OF THE MONOPOLISTS

*The Weekly Sun, Toronto*
*April 29, 1897*

Goldwin Smith, supporter of commercial union with the United States, denounces the New Tariff.

It is related that for twelve nights after Sir Robert Peel had proposed the abolition of the Corn Laws "speaker after speaker indulged in personal recriminations. They recalled to his memory the speeches he had made in defence of the Corn Laws, and as to his assertion that he had changed his mind they denied his right to do so." Peel replied that he had yielded to the force of argument and conviction: "nor do I feel abashed at admitting that I have been in error." "I shall," he went on, "leave a name execrated by every monopolist who clamors for protection because it conduces to his own benefit, but it may be that I shall also leave a name sometimes remembered with good will in the abodes of those whose lot it is to labor and earn their daily bread by the sweat of their brow, when they shall recruit their exhausted strength with abundant and untaxed food, the sweeter because it is no longer leavened by a sense of injustice."

To compare small things with great, the scene at Ottawa is somewhat different. Speaker after speaker is throwing Mr. Laurier's promises in his teeth, but he cannot like Peel, plead that he has broken them in the interest of the masses. On the contrary, he has broken them in the interest of monopolists. The English statesman, pledged to legislate for the selfishness of the few, turned and wrecked his party in order that justice might be done to the many. The Canadian politician has been induced by evil counsellors to reverse the process. It is anything but a heroic spectacle. Canadians cannot point to it and say to their children: "Behold an example of robust virtue. There is a man with the courage to do right at any cost." We do not believe it is even good politics. He may get the support of the few, but, having gone back on the many, the many must feel disposed in the nature of things to go back on him, and, if they do, his fall will be as disastrous as Peel's was inspiriting and glorious.

## 17 CONSERVATIVE OBJECTIONS TO THE IMPERIAL PREFERENCE

*The Sarnia Observer*
*April 30, 1897*

As for Sir Charles Tupper's[1] objection that Canada should not give so much for nothing to the Mother Country, every generous hearted and even just minded Canadian will blush at the mercenary huxtering spirit which would demand of Great Britain, which gives everything to us and holds back nothing, a return involving taxation of her own citizens for the mere removal of a portion of the obstacles which we have raised against her trade with us.

[1] Tupper was Leader of the Opposition in the House of Commons.

## 18 OBJECT OF PREFERENTIAL TARIFFS: FREER TRADE

*The Monetary Times, Toronto*
*April 30, 1897*

As Great Britain taxes our produce much less than any other nation does, she is by that fact, and by that fact alone, entitled to the preference which is offered not the less to all countries that choose to avail of it. If all countries were to accept the offer, the preference would disappear; there will be preference only so long as some countries elect not to accept the conditions of the preference.

## 19 THE NEW TARIFF PROVES THE LOYALTY OF THE LIBERAL PARTY

*The Sarnia Observer*
*May 7, 1897*

In England the preferential features of the Liberal tariff has excited from all quarters the liveliest expressions of approbation and pleasure. The genuine and hearty outburst of unanimous approval in the Mother Land is a glowing tribute not only to the loyalty displayed by the Liberal party, but also to the wisdom and sagacity of the administration which has displaced the Tupper incapables of yesterday. England announces her pride in her Canadian offspring as she greets the Liberal differential tariff with such emphatic expressions of affection through the columns of her press all over the Kingdom. Kipling heralds it in appropriate verse, and Sir Charles E. H. Vincent hails it on the floors of the British parliament by notice of a resolution expressing England's grateful and paternal recognition to the government and people of Canada. As the days pass by bringing their mead of praise of the new Liberal Tariff and its loyal sentiment embodied in its declaration of preferential trade with the Mother Country, is it to be wondered at that Tories great and Tories small are dumb with amaze. Like a bolt from the clear blue sky has come the condemnation of their past policy and methods, their falsity unmasked and with one sweep of Liberal patriotism the disloyal barrier for eighteen years maintained against Great Britain by them, is levelled and the nation rejoices.

## THE MATERIAL SIDE OF A SENTIMENTAL IDEA.

JACK CANUCK—My vigorous old Friend, just take your blinder off and look at this!

*[Reproduced from J. W. Bengough:* Cartoons of the Campaign 1900, *Toronto: The Poole Publishing Company, 1900.]*

# 20 CANADIAN HOPE FOR AN EMPIRE-WIDE PREFERENTIAL SCHEME

*The Manitoba Free Press, Winnipeg*
*October 8, 1897*

### The Premier's Jubilee

In the brief telegraphic report of the Premier's speech published yesterday, there is a sentence which challenges particular attention. It reads: "The ground is now cleared for preferential trade and the question would have to be urged mainly in England." What can this mean? A full report of the speech will explain of course, but standing as it does it suggests that Great Britain is to be asked to give a preference in return for a preference. That the question is to be urged "Mainly in England" can scarcely have any other meaning. That would mean a sudden and remarkable change in the views of the first minister. He told them in England that our preference was a free gift; that we wanted nothing in return ... Are we to conclude from the sentence quoted that he and his colleagues have repented their extreme generosity, and that with Lord Salisbury, the Duke of Devonshire, and Mr. Chamberlain they are now disposed to regard with favour the policy of preference for preference? Indeed there can be no other conclusion from the words as reported. There will be sincere rejoicing throughout Canada if this is to be the new policy, notwithstanding, the fact it may involve the taking of an exceedingly sharp turn by the Ministers at Ottawa. It will be the best part of the Premier's jubilee.

# 21 CHAMBERLAIN AND PREFERENTIAL TRADE

*The Star, Montreal*
*April 4, 1900*

Those Canadians that are advocating preferential trade with Great Britain will find the greatest possible encouragement in the important speech made by Mr. Chamberlain in the British House of Commons yesterday. The Colonial Secretary while denying that he had ever advocated an imperial zollverein and opposing for the present an academic resolution in favour of representation of the colonies in the Imperial Parliament declared himself in favour of closer union between the mother country and the colonies; expressed the opinion that any demand made by the colonies just now would receive a favourable reply from Parliament; and stated his belief that the only form of fiscal union that would meet with the slightest favour would be free trade within the empire with duties against strangers. In conclusion Mr. Chamberlain remarked that any suggestion must originate with the colonies; and the remark is nothing less than an invitation to the colonies to make a suggestion to the Home Government. The whole tenor of Mr. Chamberlain's speech is calculated to astound those profound Canadian statesmen who were sure that Great Britain was so hopelessly joined to the idols of free trade that there was never any hope of the colonies obtaining preferential treatment. It is evident that the most serious obstacles to Canada obtaining a preference in the British market are to be found, not in London, but in Ottawa. Under the system of protection prevailing in most colonies, the British dependencies have an asset—something of tangible value to offer in exchange for the exclusive privilege for free trade in the British market. One of the colonies was foolish enough to barter its asset for a cheap medal issued by a moribund; just as a south seas chieftain in by gone days would sell half his kingdom for a handful of beads and a bit of looking glass. But the whole tone of Mr. Chamberlain's speech indicates that the mischief done by Sir Wilfrid is not necessarily incurable and should encourage Canadian statesmen to persevere in their efforts to secure preferential trade for Canada.

## 22 CONTRACTS FOR CANADA: THE MATERIAL BENEFITS OF IMPERIALISM

*The Globe, Toronto*
*September 1, 1900*

Ottawa, August 31.—Uniforms for her soldiers are not the sort of thing that Great Britain is likely to buy in a foreign country. A tax on their importation, therefore, would probably not be asked for by the colonies if the idea of preferential trade within the Empire were adopted by the British Government. They have formerly been supplied at home, but by reason of the kindly sentiment aroused in Britain towards Canada by the Imperial policy of the present Canadian Government the attention of the War Office has been turned to Canada. The War Office and the Indian Government have sent several orders for uniforms, greatcoats, fur caps, etc. to firms in this country, and there are now on their way from these firms to Vancouver 12,000 greatcoats, 22,000 pairs of moccasins, 1,300 fur caps, and 11,000 pairs of long stockings. These goods have been ordered by the Indian Government for the use of the troops of that portion of the Empire now in China. They will be taken by the steamer Empress of China to Shanghai and to Weihaiwei. A further order from the London War Office for 30,000 greatcoats and 50,000 kharki suits will be completed in a few days ready for shipment. It will be remembered that large shipments of hay from Canada have been made within the last year on orders from the British Government and another of 3,000 tons leaves St. John next week. All these orders go to show that there is a sentiment in every trade. The preferential policy of this government has certainly had some part in arousing this sentiment towards Canada.

## 23 A REPLY TO CONSERVATIVE CRITICS OF IMPERIAL PREFERENCE

*The London Advertiser*
*September 21, 1900*

During the election campaign of 1900 there was considerable debate on the preference between Conservatives and Liberals. Cartwright, speaking at London 19 September, 1900, angrily attacked the Conservative critics of the Fielding preference.

Sir, I can understand why these men hate preferential trade. I can understand why they hate a preference. I can understand why they hate and detest to see Liberals above all things adopt preferential trade to Great Britain. Sir, it was the best possible contrast to their own lip loyalty, to their own hypocritical deference to the British Empire. What they talked about Liberals did, and, I think that is the sting of the whole business so far as they were concerned.

## 24 SUPPORT FOR AN IMPERIAL TRADE FEDERATION

*The Globe, Toronto*
*February 14, 1901*

A Report of the British Empire League annual meeting at Ottawa, February 13.

The President (Col. George T. Denison) read the following address from Hon. George W. Ross: "I regret exceedingly that I shall not be able to attend the annual meeting of the British Empire League at Ottawa. The largest question which is likely to be very soon within the arena of Imperial politics is preferential trade within the Empire. In my opinion, the time is near at hand for extending the area of preferential trade, and including within its scope the whole empire. Our trade with other colonies is growing steadily. We are already in a position to supply many of them with the class of goods which they now purchase from foreign countries.

"If all the colonies could enter into a federation of trade with each other and with the United Kingdom, as against the world, they would be brought more closely together, commercially and politically, and if this were followed up by preferential trade on the part of the United Kingdom with the colonies, as against the world, our hold of the British markets would be strengthened, and a great impetus would be given to our industries. I observe that it is stated in certain quarters that the colonies and the empire would be justified in imposing a small tariff against all other nations, as a nucleus of a fund for national defence, if for no other reason. On this point I cannot speak with any positive opinion, as it is a phase of preferential tariff to which I have not given full consideration. I had hoped that, with the advance of civilization, general disarmament would take place: that the arts of peace would be cultivated to such an extent as to exclude the warlike spirit of the human race. Great as has been the progress of the world in the last fifty years in other directions, I fear our progress in this direction has been very slow.

"No nation is secure that depends for its existence entirely upon the good-will of its neighbours. I fear where a nation is found to be unprepared to defend itself it is likely to become a prey to the selfishness of other nations more aggressive and more warlike, and as it is probable that this phase of our colonial relations may be discussed at the annual meeting of the League I shall all the more regret that I shall not be able to hear the views of many of our leading men upon the matter . . . ''

---

## 25 THE PREFERENTIAL TARIFF: AN END TO COLONIAL AUTONOMY?

*La Vérité, Quebec*
*April 20, 1901* [translation]

Finances and Imperialism: During the general debate on the Dominion budget, Mr. Henri Bourassa, MP for Labelle, delivered a most noteworthy speech during the March 28 sitting on Canada's finances and the imperialist movement.

The member for Labelle discussed the second suggestion from the leader of the Opposition in favor of a preferential tariff (using the currently fashionable neologism) for the whole British empire. Mr. Bourassa had no difficulty in clearly exposing the dangers to our autonomy contained in the policy of the Leader of the Opposition for a *mutual preference* in tariff matters. All he had to do was to analyze the report of the recent congress in London of the Empire's Chambers of Commerce.

That congress, made up of delegates from the main British and Colonial Chambers of Commerce, was truly astonishing. It not only discussed questions concerning the political unification of the Empire and Imperial military co-operation more than it did commercial affairs; but it was the colonial delegates who were most zealous in favor of imperialism in all its forms.

For example, a certain Mr. Macfarlane of Ottawa, a civil servant, requested that Canada be taxed at the rate of five percent on all imports, the resulting trifle of six million dollars a year to go to the British army and navy! A Mr. Geoffrion, of the Montreal Chamber of Commerce, appeared to be the only colonial delegate in favor of colonial autonomy. Without doubt remembering the fine words of Sir Wilfred Laurier who, in speaking of Canada's contribution to the South African war, had stated that Canada meant to keep her freedom, Mr. Geoffrion proposed that "the colonies not be asked to contribute to Imperial defense unless they do so voluntarily, without obligation or written law."

Well! Mr. Geoffrion could not find anyone, among the three hundred delegates, willing to support his motion which was consequently never put up to a vote!

To summarize the results of the congress: when it was a question of granting the colonies a degree of representation in the Imperial council, there were differences of opinion, when it was a question of gaining favors for the colonies from Britain, the matter was pushed aside, but when it came to taxing the colonies for the sole benefit of Britain, the congress declared itself unanimously in favor of the motion!

And not only did the British delegates not protest—that was natural enough—they didn't even say thank you!

When we come to this tariff policy of mutual preference we are playing with fire.

For if this policy ever becomes a reality, which is quite possible, colonial autonomy will be harmed; for it will be an Imperial council, sitting in London, where each individual colony will be swamped, and not the parliament of each colony, that will supervise the practical application of this mutual preference policy in tariff matters.

And once again we will be governed from Downing Street!

Many will say perhaps that colonial parliaments will always be free to accept or reject what is suggested to them and that the Imperial government will never be able to force anything on them.

Doubtlessly true, but it must not be forgotten that the Irish parliament was also free to sell or not sell the liberties of Ireland... and it sold them!

That sale was made quickly, it is true, but it did not happen more surely than is now proceeding the whittling away of Canada's autonomy!

We must thank Mr. Bourassa for having once again loudly sounded the alarm.

---

## 26 LAURIER'S AIM: TO WIDEN CANADA'S MARKETS OVERSEAS

*Le Soleil, Quebec*
*July 9, 1901* [translation]

It goes without saying that if our Prime Minister granted special favors to Britain, it was with the one intention of expanding the extent of our commercial relations with the mother-country and getting ahead of other powers in the British market.

---

## 27 A REVIEW OF IMPERIAL RELATIONS TO 1897

*The Weekly Sun, Toronto*
*July 29, 1897*

The drift of imperial relations to 1897: Goldwin Smith analyses the results of the Colonial Conference of 1897.

... Out of its [imperial federation] grave have arisen two phantoms: Fiscal union of the Empire and union of Imperial armaments. To fiscal union with differential duties, England demurs at once, refusing to give up the commercial policy which has borne her such rich fruits, and to sacrifice to her colonial trade, her trade, far exceeding the colonial in importance, with all the rest of the world. New South Wales, also refuses to depart from her policy of free trade while Victoria refuses to give up her protective duties on British goods. Nobody has yet undertaken to frame an imperial tariff or to show how the financial requirements of all these countries so widely scattered and so diverse in their interests and conditions, are to be forced into harmony with each other. Fiscal union of the Empire, it may pretty safely be said, will end in talk after doing temporary mischief by diverting our thoughts and efforts from free trade.

— — — — —

On the union of Imperial armaments a bright ray of hope fell the other day, when the British First Lord of the Admiralty announced that the Cape Colony had offered to present Great Britain with a first-rate man-of-war. His announcement, however, seems to have been premature, the project being only in the bud, while a naval expert deprecates that mode of contribution as pledging the imperial navy to the defence of the colony, and prefers colonial fortification of naval stations. Canadian Jingoes in England are making, over the champagne, magnificent offers of Canadian seamen for the Imperial navy. But Mr. Laurier knows well that he could not propose to our Parliament a grant for Imperial armaments with the slightest prospect of success. The Cape Colony or

Australia might, in return for its contribution, receive effective protection from the mother country. Canada could not. Her naval protection is the treaty forbidding the construction of armed vessels on the lakes. Naval demonstrations on our part might and probably would provoke a denunciation of that treaty. Supposing an armed flotilla to appear upon the lakes, what could that mighty ocean navy which was reviewed at Spithead do to preserve Canada from invasion?

— — — — —

Perhaps to the two phantoms already mentioned there should be added a third, colonial representation in the Imperial Parliament in favour of which both Mr. Chamberlain and Sir Wilfrid Laurier have both declared, Mr. Chamberlain proposing representation in the Lords, Sir Wilfrid in the Commons. We shall be ready to consider and discuss the scheme as soon as it assumes a definite shape: when we are told what special object the presence of these delegates is to serve, what their powers and duties are to be, how they are to be elected and appointed, and what their relations are to be to Canada on the one side and Great Britain on the other. There is no use in trying to grapple with a cloud. But one remark immediately occurs to us. A few weeks of England and a knighthood have sufficed to turn Sir Wilfrid Laurier into an ardent Imperialist, desiring to send Canadian delegates to the Imperial Parliament, and himself averring that it would be his highest ambition to be one of them, if he were not too old. How long after setting foot in England, and coming under the influences of London society, would the ordinary delegate of Canada to the British Parliament remain Canadian?

# Section III

## Canada And The Boer War, 1899-1902

# 1 CANADA HEARS OF THE JAMESON RAID

*The Globe, Toronto*
*January 1, 1896*

First news of the Jameson raid was given a minor position on the first page of the *Globe* under the news of the new poet laureate Mr. Alfred Austin and other British political news.

London, December 31—The *Morning Post* will tomorrow publish a despatch from Vienna saying that a telegram from Pretoria, capital of the Transvaal states that an armed force of the British South Africa Company numbering 800 men and armed with a Maxim and other guns is reported to have entered the Transvaal. This force is said to have reached the vicinity of Rustenburg and intends to march on Johannesburg. President Kruger has ordered that its advance be forcibly prevented and has issued a proclamation appealing to the burghers to defend their country. The despatch adds that fighting seems inevitable.

The papers here will tomorrow publish a statement emanating from a commercial source that Dr. Jameson the Administrator of the British South Africa Company has led 500 armed men into the Transvaal to assist the foreign residents of that republic to enforce their demands that they be granted equal political rights with the Boers. The papers will add that Rt. Hon. Joseph Chamberlain, Secretary of State for the Colonies, has ordered the immediate return of this force to British territory.

# 2 CRITICISM OF THE BRITISH SOUTH AFRICA COMPANY

*The Globe, Toronto*
*January 7, 1896*

In the unfortunate entanglements which have arisen in South Africa the German press is assuming an attitude which cannot be justified. With a zeal which is almost hysterical they are striving to load the British nation with the responsibility of the recent raid on the Transvaal. Britain was not behind the expedition of the South Africa Company, a fact for which both Britain and the victorious Boers have reason to be thankful. ... Britain and her colonies are able to manage their own affairs and to punish wrong doing within their domains without any advice or assistance from the restless emperor. But it would be a great mistake to allow indignation over this unwarranted interference to blind the British people to the grievous wrong which has been done in the organization of a raid against a people who, whatever their internal difficulties and differences may be, were peacefully disposed toward the colony in which it was organized.

The highest sentiments of our people, the desire to spread Christian influence and free institutions around the globe, to extend the sphere of helpful British influence, have been worked upon before today to secure support for the questionable work of trading corporations. Such deception has been rendered comparatively easy by the natural drift of the medium through which news has reached the British press. The history of our own Hudson's Bay Company is not entirely free from soiled pages. The British South Africa Company is the most influential of its kind ever organized. There is much mystery regarding its membership but its influence has often been too manifest. The smoke and dust of a conflict between Britain and Germany would hide the operations which Dr. Jameson's failure threatens to reveal. ... The failure of the joint stock company responsible for the raid and its results would be a most effectual check to a line of operations calculated to reflect anything but honour on the British nation.

# 3 WAR SPIRIT

*The Province, Vancouver*
*July 3, 1899*

The fact that the Boers have been allowed to pursue their policy of injustice and oppression so long is due solely to the magnanimity of the British Governments which have shrunk from coercing a weak power. The United States went to war with Spain because Spain oppressed her own subjects in Cuba. If the United States did right to go to war as the champion of an alien people, how much more would Britain be justified in coercing the Boers, by force of arms, into granting justice to British subjects.

*July 11, 1899*

The South African war cloud looms larger than ever in the light of today's dispatches. It will be almost a relief now when the first rifle cracks.

---

# 4  BOER TYRANNY

*The Province, Vancouver*
*July 17, 1899*

### The Limit Reached

### How British Subjects are Ruled by the Boers

For years the Uitlander has suffered under the oppression of a horde of ignorant Dutch farmers. He has been ground under the heel of tyrannical rulers, insulted, humiliated, goaded past endurance. Possessing himself in patience as exemplary as it has been enduring, he has only kicked over the traces after humble submission to a degree of oppression only to be realized by those who have experienced it. Until now he has exercised that self-restraint which is part and parcel of his nationality. Goad him beyond a certain point, and this very characteristic only renders him a more dangerous enemy.

The Transvaal republic has exceeded the breaking strain. The Uitlander remains a British [subject] still, notwithstanding his transportation to alien soil. By virtue of the English blood in his veins he is a man above all things—he has been treated like the meanest cur that ever crawled the streets. His grievances are not those of a man who cries pettishly for a vote on mere principle. By withholding the franchise, the Boer government have the power to do with him as they please, and they have transgressed their moral obligations to such an extent that it is impossible for him to tamely submit and remain an Englishman. On the other hand they will not permit him to become a Transvaal citizen.

It is he who has made the Transvaal. He defrays three-fourths of the cost of the state. He pays the piper, and he is not allowed to join in the chorus, much less set the tune. He has transferred Johannesburg from a struggling collection of wooden shanties into one of the finest cities in the world. And with the money of the defenceless Uitlander a fort that commands the whole range of the town has been built ... By means of his capital and energy and industry a valueless pastoral country is now the richest spot on earth. It has been compassed in the face of almost insuperable obstacles—prohibitive taxes, personal insult, injustice, irritating and unnecessary laws, framed for the very purpose of goading him to desperation.

The Uitlanders' children are compelled to learn a hideous Boer dialect, known as the "tool", or grow up uneducated. The English language is forbidden in the Transvaal to school children who have passed the third standard. No indignity is too great to put upon the Uitlander. Only quite recently a law was actually passed requiring Englishmen in the Transvaal to carry passes like the Kaffirs. The Boers think more of their dogs, and feed their dogs better, than their Kaffir servants ...

---

# 5  THE FIGHTING ABILITY OF THE BOERS

*The Globe, Toronto*
*September 20, 1899*

The South African situation brought out the extremes of journalism. Here the responsible Toronto *Globe* publishes a very sober, thoughtful warning that as a result of the Boer victory at Majuba Hill, 1881, they will be tough fighters. Then the next day unfounded rumours of their probable treachery were the headline on page one.

Whatever may be thought of the attitude of the British Government towards the Transvaal, it can scarcely be held that it is encouraged in assuming a menacing position because of the weakness of the adversary. No man of ordinary powers of reflection can persuade himself that the conquest of the Boers will be an easy task. The quality of their metal has already been tested...

The problem that faces Englishmen is that if a handful of rebels without means, without a government, without artillery, without money, could effect so much, what will the forces of an organized state furnished with the most modern weapons of war, with plenty of money and fighting in their own land, for their political existence be able to do? Of the eventual outcome, they are probably in no doubt, but it is evident that it is a conflict in which there can be little glory and in which there is a possibility of reverses that like Laing's Nek and Majuba Hill, it would be desirable to forget.

*September 21, 1899*

Poisoning Streams—Incredible Story that the Boers are Planning a Peculiarly Dastardly Campaign.

# 6 A CANADIAN CONTINGENT FOR SOUTH AFRICAN SERVICE?

*The Globe, Toronto*
*October 3, 1899*

The idea of sending Canadian troops abroad aroused nationalist feelings in many Canadians. Here is a Liberal view at the start of the war.

The despatch of a Canadian contingent would be in the nature of a national declaration of Canada's stake in the British Empire. The interest which the force will have in the eyes of Great Britain will be in the fact that it is Canadian. By all legitimate means this national character of the contingent should be maintained. Major-General Hutton for instance, has already broached the question of the advisability of the use of some distinctively Canadian insignia for the use of our militia, and this idea might well be carried out in the accoutrements of the contingent. What could be more appropriate for instance, than the prominent use of the Maple Leaf or the beaver as a badge or in the appointments of officers and men?...

Canadian from Colonel to drummer boy—that should be the description of the contingent we should offer to the mother country. Every person in connection with the force should be a Canadian by birth or residence; Canada's offering to the empire should set forth the good service which her sons can render in every rank.

# 7 ATTEMPTS TO FORCE LAURIER'S HAND

*The Globe, Toronto,*
*October 3, 1899*

Although Laurier had made no decision to send a contingent, the Canadian Military Gazette which had close links to General Hutton, the militia commander, announced that troops would be offered. Laurier was furious with this attempt to promote public feeling.

The Military Gazette of this city, which is in close touch with the headquarters staff in Ottawa, will say in to-day's issue:—

"If war should be commenced in the Transvaal—which seems probable—the offer of a force from the Canadian militia for service will be made by the Canadian Government. In that event an eight-company battalion of infantry, composed of 28 officers and 981 non-commissioned officers and men will be raised. Such a battalion should be made up from all over Canada by allotting a certain number of officers and men in proportion to the number of militia to each district. The battalions for the Red River expedition were organized on this basis which was found to be most satisfactory. In addition to this battalion there will be a squadron of cavalry, composed of 6 officers and 154 non-commissioned officers and men and 161 horses, and a battery of field artillery, made up of 6 guns, 5 officers, and 166 non-commissioned officers and men and 133 horses. The above strength is the war establishment of these units. . . . There is little doubt but that such a battalion would be uniformed, armed, equipped, and paid by the Canadian Government.

"As the number of troops required in the Transvaal will be limited, it is most improbable that any larger force will have an opportunity to serve.

"As the battalion of infantry will form a complete unit, and may have to act independently under its own commanding officers, great care has been exercised by the department in selecting an officer to command who would inspire confidence in those under him as well as in the Canadian public. The Government think it would be a criminal act of folly to appoint an amateur militia officer without army experience to command a battalion on service in the field, especially against such an enemy as the Boers. In this connection it is said that the command has been offered to Colonel Ivor Herbert, C.B., A.A.G., Home District, London, England, formerly in command of our militia. ... Arrangements for organizing such a force have been completed and the officers selected, so that when the order to concentrate is given, no confusion or loss of time will ensue. . . ."

# 8 THE GOVERNMENT LACKS MORAL COURAGE

*The Star, Montreal*
*October 4, 1899*

The Conservative press attacks Tarte and the Laurier Government for not sending troops to South Africa.

It is not constitutional authority that the Government lacks to send Canadian troops to the Transvaal, it is moral courage to do its duty at the risk of offending a disloyal element which objects to any that tends to strengthen the bonds which unite England and Canada.

# 9 "AND THEY STRAIGHT-WAY MADE EXCUSE"

*The Citizen, Ottawa*
*October 6, 1899*

A few of the Government organs are coming half-heartedly to the defence of the administration for its unaccountable apathy in refusing to make an offer of a Canadian contingent to Great Britain in the present crisis. That Britain expects to require a large body of troops is apparent from the news yesterday that the army corps now being prepared is to be increased to 40,000 men. It would not be so bad if the Laurier Government made an offer of a Canadian contingent. In such an event it would be speedily known whether our troops were wanted or not, but apparently the Government is determined not to make the offer, lest it might be accepted. Anticipating the instigation which the disgraceful inaction of the Government is certain to cause among all loyal Canadians, the party organs are already inventing excuses and obstacles to shield Sir Wilfrid and his colleagues from the storm of criticism which is brewing. The Ottawa *Free Press* in the course of a lengthy apology for its ministerial friends says:

> Perhaps those who clamour for the despatch of a brigade or whatever they sketch out, are evidently not aware what the cost and trouble of despatching such a force would be.

Sixty million dollars to make votes, but not a cent to keep faith with the Empire.

# 10 CANADIAN NON-INVOLVEMENT

*Le Temps, Ottawa*
*October 6, 1899* [translation]

Let those who are burning with the desire to shoulder a rifle against the Boers enlist in a British regiment ... But to demand that the Dominion cabinet take our money to organize, equip, transport and pay for such a unit, to demand further that, to make a show of its loyalty, the autonomous government of Canada fling itself on Britain's side in this war which today we do not wish to analyze, but which impartial history will one day judge, no, count us out, we shall never agree! Why should we go to the Transvaal? Either the Transvaal is an independent country, or it is a British colony. If the republic is independent, Britain has no reason to impose her orders on the internal government of that country and we have no right to get mixed up in this open wrong. If the Transvaal is a British colony the sister colonies are committing a despicable act in ganging up with the mother-country so as to crush a small people who wish to keep or win their independence: a natural goal for all colonies capable of going it alone.

Although the Liberal newspapers have as yet said nothing on the subject we feel that the government of Canada will be unable officially to take part in the African war. It cannot grab taxpayers' money for a mismanaged exhibition of imperialism which has never up till now been in the Liberal program.

# 11 THE DICTATES OF CANADIAN AUTONOMY

*The Morning Chronicle, Halifax*
*October 6, 1899*

Although most Liberal papers of English Canada supported sending troops as a demonstration of imperial unity, they were still hesitant about the constitutional difficulties which Laurier had outlined.

That the presence of Canadian and other colonial troops in South Africa in the war crisis which seems to be impending, would be a magnificent object lesson on the solidarity of the empire, is true, and we have little doubt that the great majority of Canadians will be immensely pleased if the lesson can be read out to the world; but the government of Canada cannot exceed its powers—as trustees of the Canadian people they must act with deliberation and consideration within the lines of the constitution.

# 12 IMPERIAL UNITY DEMANDS PARTICIPATION

*The Manitoba Free Press, Winnipeg*
*October 9, 1899*

As public feeling in English Canada mounted for sending a contingent to South Africa, the Liberal press calmly announced that troops would be sent in spite of Laurier's statements to the contrary.

If hostilities grow out of the present troubles in the Transvaal the Canadian Government would no doubt offer to the Imperial authorities a Canadian regiment for active service. Such a regiment should be organized and equipped at Canada's expense and should be led by a Canadian officer. If such an officer can not be found in Canada no doubt a graduate of the Canadian military college now holding a commission in an Imperial regiment could be transferred to the new Canadian regiment and given the command...

The idea of a Canadian regiment does not originate in any suggestion of need ... The idea is born of the Imperial spirit now so plainly manifested on every hand ... Some of the fighting if war breaks out would be done under conditions much better understood by Canadians and Australians than by the regular British soldier.

... To those who cherish the hope of seeing Imperial Federation accomplished in some tangible form the lack of local federation in South Africa presents an obstacle and from this as well as from other points of view it would be most appropriate for a successful federation like Canada to have a hand in removing that obstacle to a wider and magnificent federation of the British Empire.

## 13 TARTE'S "DISLOYALTY" IN OPPOSING PARTICIPATION

*The Mail and Empire, Toronto*
*October 11, 1899*

Large numbers of gallant French-Canadian officers have expressed their readiness to aid in the formation of a contingent to serve with the force in Africa. They are not to blame for the fact that Canada is not represented. Nor are the people of Quebec. The responsible parties are the ministers who have stood in the way of action.

There is no doubt that Mr. Tarte[1] is the premier of Canada.

[1]Israel Tarte was Laurier's Minister of Public Works.

## 14 THE GOVERNMENT WILL ACT

*The Globe, Toronto*
*October 11, 1899*

The Imperial authorities have all along known that the Government of Canada will gladly furnish a force for service in South Africa. It was the request of the British Government that the Canadian Administration refrained from making any public announcement as to their intentions in the event of certain things happening, but, nevertheless, the War Office well knew from despatches sent by our Government that we were ready.

*October 13, 1899*

Reports to the effect that the cabinet is not whole-minded on the subject are wholly unfounded. The correspondent of *The Globe* is in a position to state that the Government is acting completely homogeneously. That a Canadian contingent will be sent to South Africa is absolutely certain.

## 15 TARTE ACCUSED OF RACISM

*The Mail and Empire, Toronto*
*October 13, 1899*

It is clear that Mr. Tarte regarded the crisis as a new opportunity to operate his wicked race cry—the anti-British cry that he raised on behalf of Mercier in 1891 and of Laurier of 1896. ... His purpose was to split the country on the issue, to promote a division where otherwise friendship would reign, and to make party capital for himself.

## 16 A SPLIT IN THE LIBERAL RANKS

*The Spectator, Hamilton*
*October 14, 1899*

A very interesting and significant feature of the split in the Liberal ranks over the Transvaal question is the rupture between Tarte and Mayor Préfontaine M.P. of Montreal. Mr. Préfontaine is one of the most prominent members of the old guard and has never had very much use for Mr. Tarte. In fact, it has more than once been understood that Mr. Préfontaine would take Mr. Tarte's place in the cabinet if ever Sir Wilfrid was able to get rid of his master. Mr. Préfontaine is a strong friend of the premier and accompanied the latter to Chicago and returned with him. Mr. Préfontaine immediately on his arrival proceeded to place himself in direct antagonism to Mr. Tarte and declared that the time had come for Canada to redeem its pledge and show its loyalty to the empire. Mayor Préfontaine reiterated his declaration to-day. The two are likely to be more than ever at daggers drawn. Mayor Pré-fontaine's patriotic course was much commented upon to-day, and universally applauded.

## 17 TARTE: A BOER SYMPATHIZER

*The Spectator, Hamilton*
*October 16, 1899*

Laurier's eventual decision to send troops did not end the Conservative criticism.

Were the young men of Canada to resent the small-souled action of the Canadian government by refusing to enlist for Africa under the conditions forced upon them by the disloyal boss of the incompetent gang at Ottawa, it would simply gratify Tarte. He would glory in the fact that the young men of Canada had refused to go to fight his friend Oom Paul:[1] he would look upon it as an endorsement of his unpatriotic conduct...

It is simply disgraceful that these good intentions have come to naught through the opposition of one foreigner who controls the weaklings of the Canadian cabinet.

[1]"Oom Paul" was the nickname for Paul Kruger, President of the Transvaal Republic.

## 18 QUEBEC'S DUTY TO CANADA'S VOLUNTEERS

*Le Soleil, Quebec*
*October 20, 1899* [translation]

Whatever might be our opinion as Quebec-ers, individually or collectively, on the question that has unfortunately become so acrimonious as to the appropriateness or otherwise of the loyalty movement toward the mother-country, we believe that the city of Quebec has one duty alone as the Canadian troops depart. It is to hail those leaving in a manner befitting their brav-ery, self-denial and devotion.

*October 30, 1899* [translation]

All the races, all the religious beliefs of our country are represented in the ranks of your regiment and since at this moment we are gathered within the walls of the most French city of the New World you should acknowledge the large share of the French Canadian element in the warm and spontaneous outburst of loyal feelings toward Britain that has characterized your triumphal journey from Victoria to Quebec.

## 19 TARTE DEFENDS HIS POSITION

*La Patrie, Montreal*
*October 30, 1899* [translation]

Tarte is speaking at Laval. Laurier's Minister of Public Works denounces the Tory Party's fits of fanaticism.

Right now Sir Wilfred Laurier is being acclaimed as never before. Our opponents think they have found the means this time to put an end to what they call French in-fluence. Sir Charles Tupper goes around shouting, and making others shout that French-Canadians are disloyal, that Sir Wilfred Laurier, and above all Mr Tarte, are disloyal to the Empire and that in the question of sending troops to the Transvaal they have provided proof of their disloyal-ty. The Secretary of State for the Colonies, Mr. Chamberlain, was criticised in the [British] Parliamentary session just ended for having spoken out too clearly to Mr Kruger, President of the Transvaal. Mr. Chamberlain replied: "Old-style diplo-macy seems to me to have been devised in order to conceal statesmen's thoughts. I belong to the diplomacy of the new style which says aloud all it is thinking." (ap-plause) In this circumstance I shall follow Mr Chamberlain's method and I shall adopt one of the new diplomacy's methods; I shall say what I think and everything that I think.

I have all kinds of faults, I recognize and confess. But I believe there is one quality that my most stubborn opponents will not deny me: people generally know where I stand. I fight openly, my position is known. (applause)

What are the facts that we must examine today?

During the last session (I was absent in Europe for reasons that are well known to you) the House of Commons unanimously adopted a resolution of sympathy toward British citizens living in the Transvaal who did not enjoy there equal rights with the Boers. I call the electorate's attention to the fact that in the debate which took place not one Member of Parliament suggested the idea of sending troops to help England in the Transvaal in case of war. Sir Charles Tupper was in his seat as Leader of the Opposition, his colleagues surrounded him, neither he nor any other proposed the idea of sending Canadian troops to the Transvaal.

War was declared. It is not for me today to discuss the causes of the conflict.

Before leaving England around a month ago, a little more than a month, I gave an interview to two British journalists. In this interview I said that in my opinion Mr Kruger's republican government had committed a big mistake and continued to commit a big mistake in not giving British citizens equal rights with the Boers. Time went on and finally some Canadian papers began to suggest the idea of sending troops to the Transvaal.

On October 3 Sir Wilfred Laurier gave an interview to the *Globe* which I am now holding, in which he declared that since Parliament had not been consulted he did not believe that the Government had the right to send troops to the Transvaal. That is approximately what he said in the interview. On October 4, the day after Sir Wilfred Laurier's interview was published, the Colonial Secretary Mr. Chamberlain sent to the various colonies, among them the Canadian government in Ottawa, a circular in which he told them that the Imperial Government was ready to receive troops which would be sent over on condition that the cost of transporting and maintaining these troops would be borne by the Colonial governments until they got to Africa. Immediately they arrived in Africa the Imperial Government declared itself ready and anxious to pay them itself. I repeat, this dispatch was addressed from London on the 4th. I have reason to believe that it was only received in Ottawa on the 5th. Sir Wilfred Laurier had an engagement in Chicago. Ministers were scattered all over the place. Sir Wilfred Laurier returned from Chicago on the evening of the 10th, the cabinet was immediately called for the 11th, and on the 12th at 4 o'clock the order in council which acceded to the Imperial Government's dispatch was signed. Our opponents criticise us for having wasted a lot of time. I think myself that we acted very quickly in a question like this one. Have we done enough? Sir Charles Tupper believes we have not.

I repeat, the Imperial Government asked us to pay the travel and maintenance expenses of our volunteers until they arrived in Africa—no more. Sir Charles Tupper believes we are disloyal because we did not say, disregarding the wish and desire of the Imperial Government: "The Canadian people is far richer than the Empire, much more powerful than Great Britain, we shall pay for everything." Right now he denounces us, he says that we are disloyal because we did not say: "No we will pay no attention to the desire of the Imperial Government, but we will do more." Well, we are prepared to submit to your judgement on this point. There are people who used to be called more Catholic than the Pope. Sir Charles Tupper wishes to be more loyal than the Queen. The rest of us, sworn servants of the Queen, are happy to be as loyal as she, and we are sure that is completely sufficient. (applause)

But the question has wider implications than a mere matter of money. I do not hide from you that I have thought a long time before making up my mind about this. This is a free colony which has hitherto lived in peace and which has developed in an orderly and progressive manner. It has never in the past been thought that Canada should participate in the Empire's wars. I am a conservative with twenty years of experience and I declare here that the opinion of Sir John A. Macdonald, the opinion of Sir Charles Tupper and of the different Conservative ministers who succeeded them was always against a policy which would make Canada take part in Imperial conflicts. I take full responsibility for my words and I shall show one of the sources where the proofs of my assertion can be found.

In 1885 England was engaged in a very difficult war in the Sudan. General Laurie who is now an MP in the British House of Commons and the late Colonel Williams offered to organize two Canadian regiments at Canada's expense. Lord Lansdowne, who was then Governor General consulted Sir John A. Macdonald, the Prime Minister of this country—an English Prime Minister if I am not mistaken—and Sir John replied in writing that Canada's policy could not be to take part in the Empire's wars.

Sir Charles Tupper himself on different occasions before the Imperial Federation League and elsewhere spoke out clearly against participation in the Empire's wars. It is very easy, as Mr. Tom Chase Casgrain was saying the other day, to sing God Save The Queen. We sing it with love and devotion, we are loyal subjects of the Queen, thank God. It is easy to play a role, as Sir Charles and Mr. Hugh Graham are playing right now in giving guarantees to an insurance company wanting to make some publicity for itself. But a country's future is not decided in this way, nor is it the way that a government, understanding its duty, makes up its mind to act.

### No Participation Without Representation

I say that if Canada and the British colonies must be summoned to take part in the Empire's wars they must have the right to representation and a vote in the councils of the Empire. The first right of a British subject is not to pay taxes without the right of a vote, without being represented. But this is precisely why at this moment Britain is at war in the Transvaal. What are the reasons given by Mr Cham-

berlain to the civilized world for invading this republic? It is, he says, and rightly, "because British subjects who pay taxes in the Transvaal do not have the same rights as those who govern the Transvaal." I repeat that if this British colony, this free colony must take part in the Empire's wars, we must have the right to take part in its councils.

I am ready to discuss this question first thing tomorrow. The British Empire and its colonies in one great military federation would be a magnificent and powerful spectacle. But as for turning the clock back one hundred years, as for agreeing to the principle that the colonies are morally or otherwise obliged to supply money, to supply troops, without having a word to say, for my part I will never take that responsibility. I repeat, and may my words be clearly understood by my compatriots, my friends, and my opponents. I am ready to discuss this question first thing tomorrow. I am the first French Canadian member of the Imperial Federation League. Let someone show me in the records of this association a single line, a single page where the colonies are asked for troops without at the same time giving them the right to vote. Sir Wilfred Laurier and a good number of us here would not be out of place in the British House of Commons. I appeal to that country "No taxation without representation"—and it shares my opinion. (applause)

### Why a Race Question?

Some have wanted to make this a race question. Why? Because Sir Wilfred Laurier is the Prime Minister of this country and because my name is Joseph Israel Tarte, Minister of Public Works, and because I am French. Sir John never sent troops to the Empire's wars. Was he attacked? Sir Charles Tupper was a minister for 25 years. But we are French. People attack us because they believe themselves in a position to be able to smother us with these accusations of disloyalty. If, instead of being French, Sir Wilfred Laurier had been English we would have had none of this racket now going on.

69

I regret, Mr. Speaker, that Sir Charles Tupper, whom I hold in affection, for he was one of my leaders, I regret that he is devoting the last years of his life, of a career now coming to an end, to stirring up religious and racial hatreds in this country. He is 79 years old, I admire his strength and energy. But instead of seeking to divide our citizens, instead of seeking to create national and religious hatreds, why does he not devote his eloquence toward cementing unity and peace between the different races living in Canada?

---

## 20 LOYAL SENTIMENTS FROM THE MAYOR OF MONTREAL

*The Herald, Montreal*
*October 31, 1899*

While the Conservative press denounced Tarte, the Liberal press emphasized the stand of Mayor Préfontaine of Montreal, a Liberal M.P. who supported sending the contingents. The following extract is part of Préfontaine's speech to the departing troops.

This is a moment of lively satisfaction, but of great solemnity for me. As the chief magistrate of this great city of Montreal it is my proud privilege to appear here on behalf of the three hundred thousand citizens of one of the most progressive cities of that glorious empire on which the sun never sets, to bid God speed to a contingent of her brave citizen soldiers, who have volunteered their services for the defence of the flag of Britannia in far away Africa. There is much glory for Montreal in being privileged to contribute so many of her plucky sons for the force so gallantly maintaining the cause of Britain and of justice in South Africa, and your fellow citizens are especially proud of you, who have so promptly responded to the call to arms. We are equally proud of you, those of your fellow citizens of French origin no less than those of English speech.

For are we not all members of one community, enjoying the same privileges and liberties and sharing the same responsibilities under the same glorious old flag? All Montrealers revere that flag, because it stands for them as the symbol of almighty protecting power, which has never failed them and which guarantees them the enjoyment of unlimited freedom.

It is a far-away cry from Montreal to South Africa, but we citizens of Canada's commercial metropolis, know very well that any loss of prestige suffered by the flag of Britain in Africa must result in a reduction of that powerful protection under which the city and the country have so mightily progressed.

The British lion is the Canadian beaver's natural protector but the protected owes a duty to the protector, and is now showing that it is ready to pay the debt in something more tangible than mere sentimental attachment.

---

## 21 THE EMPIRE IS ONE

*The Morning Chronicle, Halifax*
*November 2, 1899*

British reverses in the early months of the war intensified the imperial feeling of English Canada.

There can be no doubt that in many years no event has stirred Halifax so deeply and sympathetically as the recent reverse to a portion of General White's army at Ladysmith a few days ago. Previous British wars seemed to be far away from the Canadian people and reverses and losses were generally regarded with a certain degree of indifference, the sympathy or anxiety awakened being confined largely to the military and their immediate friends. Things are different now. We are interested parties—partners with the mother country in the work of the empire.

---

## 22  A KIPLING POEM ON BOER TYRANNY

*The Methodist Magazine and Review,*
*Toronto*
*November, 1899*

### The Old King

All we have of freedom—all we use or
   know—
This our fathers bought us, long and long
   ago,
Ancient Right unnoticed as the breath we
   draw—
Leave to live by no man's leave, under the
   Law.

Lance and torch and tumult, steel and
   grey-goose wing,
Wrenched it, inch and ell and all, slowly
   from the King;
Till our fathers 'stablished, after bloody
   years,
How our King is one with us, first among
his peers.

So they bought us freedom—not at little
cost—
Wherefore must we watch the King, lest
   our gain be lost,
Over all things certain, this is sure indeed:
Suffer not the old King; for we know the
   breed!

Here is nought unproven—here is naught
   to learn,
It is written what shall fall, if the King
   return;
He shall mark our goings; question whence
   we came,
Set his guards about us, all in Freedom's
   name.

He shall take his tribute, toll of all our
   ware,
He shall change our gold for arms—arms
   we may not bear;
He shall break his judges; if they cross his
   word,
He shall rule above the Law, calling on the
   Lord.

He shall heed our whispers, for the night
   shall bring
Watchers 'neath our window, lest we mock
   the King—
Hate and all division; host of hurrying
   spies;
Money poured in secret, carrion breeding
   flies.

Strangers of his council, hirelings of his
   pay,
These shall deal our Justice; sell, deny,
   delay;
We shall drink dishonour, we shall eat
   abuse—
For the Land we look to—for the Tongue we
use.

We shall take our station, dirt beneath his
   feet,
While his hired captains jeer us in the
   street;
Cruel in the shadow, crafty in the sun,
Far beyond his borders shall his teaching
   run.

Sloven, sullen, savage, secret, uncon-
   trolled—
Laying on a new land evil of the old;
Long-forgotten bondage, dwarfing heart
   and brain—
All our fathers died to lose he shall bind
   again.

Step by step and word by word; who is
   ruled may read.
Suffer not the old Kings—for we know the
   breed—
All the right they promise—all the wrong
   they bring.
Stewards of the Judgement, suffer not the
   King!

   Rudyard Kipling, in the London *Times*.

Mr. Kipling's parable very clearly sets
forth the wrongs of the Outlanders, the
crimes of the tyrannical oligarchy, mis-
named the Transvaal Republic. The
patience of Britain has been strained to the
breaking point. Dreadful as the alternative
of battle and bloodshed is, it cannot, we
think, be said that Britain has gone into
this conflict wantonly, or with a light heart.

Possibly there is room for criticism as to some of the acts of Mr. Chamberlain, certainly there is for the reckless Jameson Raid; but these in no degree condone the flagrant wrongs, tyrannies, and oppression of the South African Republic. Up to the very last Britain was anxious for the peaceful settlement of the long-standing grievances of the Outlanders. Kruger's insolent ultimatum flung the sword into the scales. Now at very great cost of treasure and of blood these wrongs must be righted, and the same liberties secured for Britons beyond the Vaal as are enjoyed by the Dutch at the Cape.

It is the veriest nonsense, if not hypocrisy, for the Boers to claim that they are fighting the battles of freedom. They are very fond of liberty, says Mr. Garrett, a member of the Cape Assembly, so fond of it that they wish to keep it all themselves. On the other hand nothing is more manifest than that in this conflict, to use the words of the premier of Canada, "Great Britain stands in defence of a holy cause, in the defence of holy justice, for the defence of the oppressed, for the enfranchisement of the down-trodden, and for the advancement of liberty, progress and civilization."

# 23 THE DIVINE MISSION OF THE EMPIRE

*The Globe, Toronto*
*November 6, 1899*

*The Globe prints a sermon from the Rev. Professor Clark, a Toronto divinity professor, who sees British imperialism as the agent for the forces of righteousness in world affairs.*

England was now doing for the subject races in South Africa what she had been doing for subject races in all parts of the world...

For weeks and months, the Boer Government had been playing with the government of Great Britain, preparing their resources that they might strike at us at a moment when we were not prepared.

Nothing had been wanting in patience and forbearance on the part of the British Government...

If God were with us we would be sure to succeed, and the bloodshed and sacrifices would not have been given in vain for the work which we believed we were called upon by God to do...

The work they (the British and Colonial soldiers) had taken in hand was a work for human civilization, for the progress of the race of man in intelligence, self-control and liberty in all things that make men great and good. There were two great forces in the world, one helping the forward movement, the other force in favour of ignorance, bondage, and servitude. None could think of the power with which they were in conflict as a power standing for civilization. Any additional power given this republic was a power against the human race.

The work that England had undertaken was a work for us all. Livingstone in Africa recognized the importance of the work of the gospel. It was not merely to teach religion but was to raise men out of their ignorance and bondage to teach self-control freedom and intelligence. Until men had come to know Almighty God there was little chance of them becoming emancipated. We should therefore support strongly the work of the Empire. We should do our own part, bear our own sacrifices and accept them as being placed upon us by God for His glorification and the benefit of humanity.

# 24 CANADA: AN EXAMPLE OF RACIAL EQUITY?

*The Spectator, Hamilton*
*November 20, 1899*

*Feeling against French language rights flows over into editorial analysis of imperial affairs.*

*It is said that Lord Salisbury intends to consult the colonial premiers as to the settlement to be made in South Africa after the war. One of the most valuable examples of the settlement of a race ques-*

*tion is to be found in Canada. In fact, this settlement might be regarded as perfect if it were not for the false alarms which were raised in the province on the slightest pretext.—Toronto Globe.*

In fact the "settlement" has been most imperfect: it is very little, if any, better than no settlement at all. The French language is the national language of Quebec; it is employed in the schools from which English is strictly excluded; history is falsified and Montcalm is the hero and Wolfe the despicable foreigner. The result of the stupid mistake in perpetuating the French language is seen in the fact that today, a century and a half after the conquest, Quebec is as French as she was then, and has made as little progress in almost everything as she has toward becoming British. Quebec is an old-world, behind-the-time, unprogressive colony planted in the midst of an enterprising and progressive people, an eyesore, a bar to progress, and a discredit to the foolish Englishmen who made the compact 150 years ago. Every British Canadian knows these to be facts; the *Globe* knows them to be facts, and many and many a time the old *Globe* has stated them as facts in language which could not be misconstrued. But the new French alliance of the Grit party; the fact that the government is in the hands of Frenchmen, prevents the *Globe* of to-day from acknowledging the truth.

## 25 ANGLO-SAXON CULTURAL IMPERIALISM

*La Vérité, Quebec*
*November 28, 1899* [translation]

One of the complaints of the British in the Transvaal is that the Transvaalers persist in maintaining the Dutch language as their national tongue and teaching it in schools. They would like to substitute English in place of the Boers' national language. It is really funny to see certain Anglo-Saxons, in America as much as in Europe, preach the doctrine that no civilization can exist without the English language. They are so much in love with themselves that they cannot see how ridiculous they are.

## 26 THE ADMONITIONS OF GEORGE GRANT

*The Citizen, Ottawa*
*November 28, 1899*

George Monro Grant, principal of Queen's University, Kingston, was one of the few voices of moderation in English Canada. He warns of the influence of Cecil Rhodes and the capitalists.

Kingston, Ontario, November 27—Principal Grant, who sympathized with the Boers while they were arguing their cause, has naturally changed his opinion, a new issue being presented. The ultimatum of the Transvaal Government, he said tonight, was insolent and positively childish. The crisis was met in a spirit worthy of the best days of the British people. The principal commended the spirit displayed by the colonies. The war had demonstrated that the British empire feels itself more a living unity than ever before. It has been forced into a fight and the fight was for liberty, justice and civilization. If the war had not been entered upon it would have permitted the triumph in South Africa of primitive conceptions of life and an inferior ideal of society. The principal hopes that whatever the future settlements of South Africa may be, nothing shall be done to place the base elements in the saddle. The base elements are represented by Cecil Rhodes and the mining capitalists generally. The principal agreed with much the Hon. I. J. Tarte had said: "It would never do as a rule to allow a government to commit us to a war without the consent of parliament or to spend money before any discussion has taken place on the subject," he said. "It is also quite true that if it is to be our policy, as I think it should be, to take part in imperial affairs, we should understand the principles that should regulate our participation and to this a thorough discussion in parliament is indispensable." I think that all who are interested in parliamentary government and in imperial federalism should be grateful to him.

## 27 FRANCOPHILE SENTIMENTS?

*L'Évangéline, Weymouth, N.S.*
*December 9, 1899* [translation]

The Boers are for the most part French by descent, and although they are Protestant and Dutch-speaking, they still have easily recognizable French names.

## 28 A DISILLUSIONED CANADIAN

*The Canadian Magazine, Toronto*
*December, 1899, p.193*

A jaundiced comment from the editor of the *Canadian Magazine.*

It is difficult to write of "Peace on earth goodwill towards men" when both branches of the Anglo-Saxon people are engaged in subduing inferior races ... Let us therefore hope that when the Boer and the Filipino have been made to realize that the Anglo-Saxon race never errs, that it makes war only for the benefits of humanity, a more secure peace shall be assured and the gospel of the Fatherhood of God and the brotherhood of man shall have a wider scope for its beneficent rule.

## 29 THE HYPOCRISY OF LAURIER

*La Vérité, Quebec*
*December 11, 1899* [translation]

This very same Sir Wilfred who speaks in so fierce a manner of justice and religious freedom ... in Africa, tells us with angelic calmness that the Manitoba Schools question has been settled. This exterminator of the Boers is tremendously long sighted. For him to detect an injustice it must be 8,000 miles away.

## 30 THE POWER OF JOSEPH CHAMBERLAIN

*The Canadian Magazine, Toronto*
*December, 1899, p. 144*

Here the role of Joseph Chamberlain, the British Colonial Secretary, in forging a military alliance of the empire, is warmly applauded. Note the lack of interest in Canadian autonomy.

In 1891, in addressing an Imperial Federation deputation, Lord Salisbury is reported to have said that a united empire means a union for customs and a union for war. The union for war has come, suddenly, swiftly. Six months ago we were not thinking of it, to-day it is an accomplished fact. The man who did the deed was the Rt. Hon. Joseph Chamberlain. He knew and understood the colonies; he called and they responded. If certain colonial premiers and colonial cabinets hesitated, the Colonial Secretary knew how to force their hands. The people who imagine that the Secretary for the Colonies does not hold those colonies in the hollow of his hand, have not read the inside history of the present crisis. He is above politics and can occasionally make and unmake politicians even at Ottawa.

## 31 CANADIAN INTERESTS AT STAKE

*La Presse, Montreal*
*December 19, 1899* [translation]

The Second Contingent.

It is no longer a matter of security for our Sovereign's armed forces, it is now in the midst of danger the protection of our bodies that we must offer. We well know our role, it is to save the situation. No more theorising, no more political discussions: one watchword alone: "we must."

French Canadians can appreciate as other nationalists the worth of British prestige, now it is our war that we shall be conducting in Africa.

Right now there is no time to lose, we must move as fast as possible. Canada's interests are so tied to the strength of the British name that, since the recent reverses, our entire financial position has been overturned, and we have grounds to fear a series of catastrophes may be imminent. Since the beginning of this war all our new business have been paralysed; it will certainly not be possible to start others up and we accept the judgement of our most reputable business men who tell us they are absolutely defenseless. This worry has perhaps not yet made itself felt among the population, but it has certainly affected the important class of traders in negotiable securities. This morning at the Stock Exchange there is only talk of ruin after yesterday's stock collapse.

## 32 FRENCH-CANADIAN CRITICISM OF BRITAIN

*L'Évenément, Quebec*
*December 23, 1899* [translation]

The great majority of French Canadians of the Province of Quebec do not approve Britain's motives for taking up arms against the small Transvaal republic. They are not alone in this opinion and a large number of Englishmen have condemned in unequivocal terms the conduct of the British Government.

## 33 THE INEVITABILITY OF THE BOER WAR

*The Manitoba Free Press, Winnipeg*
*January 1, 1900*

Canadians generally accepted the theory that the war had been caused by a conspiracy of the Boer Republics to destroy the British position in South Africa.

It is becoming more and more established by the testimony of competent and fair-minded men who can speak of their own knowledge regarding conditions in the Transvaal during recent years that the war was inevitable, that the Boers had

long been preparing for it at a cost of many millions wrung from the Outlanders and the purpose behind their preparations was the destruction of British rule in South Africa and the setting up of Boer rule in its place....

The racial hatred which is the main impulse driving the Boers in this war, made the struggle one which no human power could have avoided for long. The unfortunate magnanimity of Great Britain laid the foundation for the working out of the plans of Presidents Kruger and Steyn, Secretary Reitz and their confederates in the design of establishing a great South African Republic...

## 34 LOYALTY: A STRICT DUTY FOR CATHOLICS

*The Star, Montreal*
*January 17, 1900*

Public letter from Archbishop Bégin of Quebec to Archbishop Bruchesi of Montreal which replies to the charge of French Canadian disloyalty. It would appear to be both an explanation of the historic role of French Canada and a directive to the flock. Loyalty is the strict duty of every Roman Catholic.

As may easily be seen, history has repeated itself from the cession of Canada to our days, and it will repeat itself so long as there will be a Catholic bishop in our Canada. Our friends seem at times to forget this. Loyalty for the children of the Church of Christ is not a matter of sentiment, or of personal interest, it is a serious and strict duty of conscience, derived from a sacred principle, immutable, eternal as the Divine Lawmaker. Let them therefore, reassure themselves as regards the attitude of the Catholic clergy on similar occasion: the past has been beyond attack, the future will likewise be so, because our Catholic principles never change.

As a matter of fact, I have no hesitation in saying that it would be impossible to find, even among the highest of England's aristocracy, a succession of men, who have been more loyal than the bishops, the clergy of Quebec...

## 35 CANADA HAS COME OF AGE

*The Free Press, Ottawa*
*January 31, 1900*

The new nationality born at Confederation reaches its manhood with the Boer War and Imperialism.

The Session of Parliament which will be opened tomorrow will be of a character without parallel in the history of Canada. The session which opened on November 6, 1867, was important as signifying the birth of that new nationality to which reference was made at the time. Thirty-three years later Parliament will for the first time assert its place as part and parcel of the Empire, bearing a part in a foreign war, and sharing the cares and the responsibilities of the Imperial connection. The "new nationality" has reached its manhood's stage, and in future its relations to the Empire and conditions will be changed.

## 36 LAURIER CAUGHT BETWEEN SCYLLA AND CHARYBDIS

*The Evening Recorder, Brockville*
*February 7, 1900*

The Liberal press accused the Tories of attacking Laurier in Ontario for his disloyalty and in Quebec for his imperialism.

Unmoved by the cry of disloyalty raised against him in Ontario at the instigation of the leader of the Opposition or the cry of super-Imperialism raised against him in Quebec at the instigation of the same person for the accomplishment of the same purpose Sir Wilfrid has proceeded on the statesmanlike lines of a patriot in all this affair. His efforts to maintain peace and goodwill among all classes in spite of the wicked attempt of the Tupperites to create discord or dissension on lines of race and creed for party's sake, ought to succeed in this enlightened day, and the welfare of the country demands that it succeed.

## 37 "THE WAR IN MONTREAL": McGILL v. LAVAL

*The Free Press, Ottawa*
*March 3, 1900*

Partly as a result of the inflammatory statements in the English and French press of Montreal, there were several nights of disturbances in early March in that city. McGill students, celebrating the relief of Ladysmith, demonstrated in front of the Montreal branch of Laval University and the offices of *Le Journal, La Patrie,* and *La Presse.* When the Laval students organized a counter demonstration and ethnic feeling intensified, there was general disorder and rioting. Rival groups, no longer just of students, confronted one another with the Union Jack or the Tricolor.

Lieut.-Col. Sherwood, chief of the Dominion Police, Ottawa, and Lieut.-Col. White, District Officer commanding the Fifth Military District of this city, had a conference with the city police authorities this morning, and it was decided to mobilize the police and militia forces in order to have them in readiness for tonight in case there should be any trouble between English and French, as is greatly feared as the result of insults offered to the British flag last night by Frenchmen.

Fourteen rioters appeared in Recorder's court this morning and were fined $2 or 15 days.

The students of Laval University, and many French Canadian citizens of Montreal, held a counter demonstration last night to that given by the students of McGill. They paraded the streets, singing the Marseillaise and cheering themselves hoarse. The Union Jack was torn from the Star Building. There were several fights between the police and the students. The Victoria Rifles were called out by Col. White, D.O.C., to protect the drill shed when a disturbance was threatened.

*The Globe, Toronto*
*March 3, 1900*

Laval Men Make a Counter Demonstration
in Montreal

————

*FLAG TORN DOWN*

————

Race Feeling Growing to a Dangerous Pitch

————

*(Special Despatch to The Globe.)*

Montreal, March 1.—The anti-French campaign conducted by a number of Conservative papers for months past had its natural effect in inflaming thoughtless minds and inducing the outrages of which the McGill students and their followers were guilty towards their French-Canadian fellow-citizens yesterday. If it had been an ordinary students' outburst the whole affair would have been passed over, like others before, but coming on top of this constant baiting of everything French it has left a decided irritation, which will be long in dying. Now that the enthusiasm has blown over there is general regret at the excesses of the McGill men, who invaded private property to compel the hoisting of flags, and at the retaliation of the Laval men, who tore them down and cheered for the Queen, to show that they could be loyal without coercion … It turned out at the Police Court this morning that of the five young men arrested for creating a disturbance not one was a McGill student. Recorder Weir, in dismissing the cases, said it was natural to rejoice under the circumstances, but added that the demonstration was carried too far. Such events showed the extreme peril of newspapers raising race prejudices. French-Canadians and English-Canadians were fighting side by side in the Transvaal. French-Canadian gallantry was amply shown by those who had died and been wounded in defence of the empire. He hoped the difficulty would pass away and suggested that on the occasion of the next victory or when the war was over, a grand demonstration be made by Laval and McGill together.

### The Patrie's Opinion

*The Patrie,* referring to the disturbances yesterday says that they were the result of the appeals to passions by Tory papers, especially *The Star, Mail and Empire, News* and *Spectator,* which for months past hurled charges of disloyalty at French-Canadians. Having recalled the attack upon Lord Elgin in 1849 because he did justice to French-Canadians, *The Patrie* says that they are in the majority here, and if they wished could take revenge for these insults. "We do not advise this anti-national policy," says the *Patrie,* "but we do advise organization for vigorous resistance to such scenes. Our fellow-countrymen have the duty of compelling respect for their persons and property, by force if necessary. In truth, if this thing is to continue, if the invasion and destruction of our houses and property is tolerated, this country would soon become uninhabitable. Is it not a painful spectacle to find that we are, so to say, within two steps of civil war? We are not the aggressors, but we are strong enough to fear no one. We do not hold the majority of the English people of Montreal and of the country responsible for the shameful scenes which dishonoured our streets yesterday. We have reached a decisive hour. Confederation can be maintained only if the two races live in harmony side by side. Very little added to what has just taken place would tear to pieces the Federal agreement without much delay."

### Another Students' Riot.

Late this afternoon the Laval students started out on the march. It was reported that they were going to McGill, and the police authorities hastened a couple of posses of police there to protect the property. The students, however, turned off at Philips square and marched east again to Laval. Tonight they started out a second time and halted in front of *The Star* office on St. James street. While the body of students sang French airs one of them climbed to the roof of the temporary offices and tore down the Union Jack floating from the flagpole there. Half a dozen police stood by but did nothing. The students and a mob of followers next marched around to *The Herald* office and broke a couple of windows. From there they returned to Laval. In the meantime the McGill students, hearing that the others were on the way up, lined along the grounds and remained there for a couple of hours, but fortunately there was no conflict. They promised the professors they would not leave the grounds, and whiled away the time singing, a particular favorite being "Nearer, My God, to Thee." The Laval students on their way home stopped at the Drill Shed and tried to hoist the tri-color. The caretaker turned the hose on them and they departed. In the meantime the militia authorities had become alarmed for the safety of the hall. It happened that the Victoria Rifles had a smoking concert in their armory uptown, and Lieut.-Col. White, D. O. C., telephoned there for them to proceed to the Drill Shed. Fortunately, their services were not required. It is time, however, that the police authorities put a stop to this rowdyism for a few of them could easily have dispersed the mob tonight before mischief was done.

---

# 39  THE VOICE OF REASON

*La Presse, Montreal*
*March 5, 1900* [translation]

The Events of Last Week: Arising out of an accident the McGill escapade is now no more than an incident. We do not share the gloomy forebodings of those rightly shocked, then disturbed individuals who see in Thursday's demonstration a long drawn out plot with sinister intentions on the part of our English fellow citizens. Unprepared for this shock, French Canadians were deeply affected by it, we admit; they would be unworthy of political life if they had felt nothing.

But the first feelings of anger are now over, and the McGill students having, both themselves and through their professors, made suitable excuses which honorable men can accept and have accepted, we can now analyse the situation more coolly.

If there existed at this time violent national or religious rivalries, if some radical measure demanded a decisive solution we could understand why there should be violent aggression on one side and desperate resistance on the other. But nothing of the kind in fact exists, for imperialism, which has been talked about for twenty years, has not yet become a burning issue. Unfortunately the annoying manoeuvres of politics, although not generally dangerous, have provoked the naive and disinterested enthusiasm of our youth. Full of energy, full of courage, full of illusions, they are as yet unaware of the trickeries of that treacherous game where two parties alone control the pieces on the chess-board.

The English newspapers who have been carping for six months at French Canadian disloyalty don't believe a word of it themselves but the chance to demolish a French Prime Minister is too fine not to give it a try. This criticism is above all directed at the *Star* because it has never missed a chance to belittle French Canadians.

Thus, so as to turn the electorate against Sir Wilfred Laurier, he is accused of presiding over a province of traitors. None doubts that the McGill students, who do not read the French papers, have unconsciously absorbed this mistaken doctrine. That is why, when they went out the other day with the simple idea of celebrating, they suddenly, in a burst of budding patriotism while reading the signs on St. James street, caught a glimpse of the rebel battlements through the storm's downpour.

And, in a parallel direction, the Liberal press did not by any means turn the other cheek. With the same vigor and unfairness it denounced Sir Charles Tupper as the long-time persecutor of French Canadians; the Tories as Catholic-killers; the English provinces, whipped up by alleged incendiary speeches, as wild beasts ready to devour Quebec. Our fellow French Canadians have certainly come to feel a strong resentment against people depicted to them as so dangerous and so thirsty for our blood.

And this is why two races who have been living in peace beside each other for fifty years now suddenly find themselves glowering at each other ...

# 40 PARLIAMENT DISCUSSES THE RIOTS

*The Citizen, Ottawa*
*March 6, 1900*

The day in the house was given over entirely to discussion of the Montreal students' demonstrations of last week, or rather to the incendiary article in Mr. Tarte's paper, based upon those unfortunate but evidently much exaggerated occurrences. Both the tone and temper of the debate were unexceptionable until Mr. Tarte himself rose and opening up the floodgates of his peculiar style of oratory, proceeded to deal out what defence he could for the scandalous attitude of his paper. It takes Mr. Tarte to condemn the imaginery racial appeals of his opponents and justify his own most inflammatory philippics in the same breath. But he made rather a poor job of it yesterday. The fact that *La Patrie* on the very day of the demonstration in front of its office published a thoroughly sensible comment on the situation yet the day following, declared with grave threatenings of reprisal, that the whole affair was an attack upon the French race in Canada, that we were within two steps of civil war, and that the compact of confederation was liable to be torn up at any moment, showed too plainly the fine roman hand of the Minister of Public Works at its old tricks. As a persistent agitator of racial and creed prejudices the Minister of Public Works is without peer in Canada.

# 41 ISRAEL TARTE MEETS BOER EMISSARIES

*The Star, Montreal*
*April 4, 1900*

Israel Tarte, Laurier's Minister of Public Works, met the Boer emissaries in Europe, much to the annoyance of the British Foreign Office. The meeting was reported by the *Star's* own London correspondent. Tarte at the time made several trips between London and Paris.

Mr. Tarte's speech at the Society of Arts yesterday has created some comment, especially his advice as a French Canadian son of a rebel of 1837, to the Boers, to accept the benefits of British self-government. Mr. Tarte could probably have created a still greater sensation had he detailed his long chat with Dr. Leyds, diplomatic representative of the Transvaal, at Monsieur Delcassé's reception at Paris on Saturday. Mr. Tarte says he found Dr. Leyds most pleasant and most anxious to hear about the French Canadians. Mr. Tarte explained the liberality and freedom of British rule in French Canada, and according to his own statement added: "Now, Mr. Leyds I am the son of a rebel and I tell you you'll be beaten; you'll be crushed. If you're wise you and your people will do as we did, and enjoy the freedom we enjoy." Dr. Leyds it is added seemed much impressed.

# 42 ANTI-IMPERIALISM IN OUR SCHOOLS

*The Canadian Magazine, Toronto*
*June, 1900*

School children who questioned British or American imperialism provoked this sarcastic editorial from John A. Cooper, Editor of the *Canadian Magazine*.

Our friends in the republic have statesmanlike school-children even if their legislators and administrators cannot be accused of possessing such a virtue. The children of Philadelphia and New York, recognizing that the Cubans and Filipinos and Boers are fighting for their freedom with the hated Anglo-Saxon oppressor, decided to send a message of sympathy to President Kruger at Pretoria. They signed a long sheet of paper with several thousand names, hired a messenger boy and sent him off amid great rejoicing. This generous act shows what education is doing for the young in the United States.

And Canada is not behind. The children of Windsor, Ontario are getting up a similar message of sympathy to be sent to Aguinaldo. We cannot afford to be laggards in such grand and noble work. All honour to the children of Windsor, Ontario! Kruger would be a national hero in the United States, and, therefore, why not Aguinaldo in Canada? We are housing the Doukhobor, and Galician, the Pole, Dr. Barnardo's boys, and all the European outcast classes, why should we not offer an asylum to this hero of a thousand battles in the Philippines?

When we have offered Aguinaldo this, the world will know that there are at least two fool-nations on the North American continent.

---

# 43   THE ORANGE LODGE SUPPORTS THE WAR EFFORT

*The Free Press, Ottawa*
*June 1, 1900*

The Orange Order which had weakened in its commitment to the Conservative Party over the Manitoba Schools issue in 1896 returned strongly to the Tory fold for the election of 1900 because of the Boer War and imperialism. Here Mr. C. Wallace, Grand Master of the Order, speaks in London to the Grand Lodge.

Reflect upon what would be our position to-day had the people of this country not driven Sir Wilfrid Laurier to abandon the policy he deliberately determined upon and formally proclaimed, the policy of non-participation in the defence of the Empire, save only when Canada is attacked. We should be beneath the contempt of the whole world, the worse than contempt of brother Britons in all parts of the Empire. A more despicable doctrine has never been propounded by public man than that Canada should accept the sacrifices of the Motherland, the protection of her army and navy to maintain the integrity of the Dominion, and then, like a poltroon, refuse to contribute one dollar or one man to uphold the unity of the Empire. Thank God the miserable doctrine of Sir Wilfrid Laurier was no sooner uttered than the people of all parties arose in indignant might, and compelled him to play the patriot's part, however distasteful the task might be, or give way to men whose loyalty would be above suspicion, and who, in the day of the Empire's need, would at all hazards respond to the call for aid.

---

# 44   CANADIANS IN ACTION

The excerpt printed below is taken from
E.W.B. Morrison, *With the Guns in South Africa* (Hamilton: Spectator Printing Company, 1901), pp.88-89.
Reports from the front were given great prominence in the papers. The Hamilton *Spectator* published theirs in book form after it had appeared in the newspaper. Morrison was a journalist and reported regularly for his paper and the Ottawa *Citizen* while a member of D Company, Royal Canadian Artillery.

The swift and daring advance of this mobile mounted force which could detach smaller flying columns in any direction, struck terror into the rebels, who had not bargained for such vigorous and active measures for their dispersion. Being essentially cowardly when the odds are even, they hastened to return to the role of peaceful ranchers without offering any organized resistance to the keen, quick moving Canadians and Australians for whom the desert had no terrors, and who were ready at a moment's notice to make dashes of 40 to 50 miles in any direction from the line of march if any enemy developed in force to oppose the Queen's authority. If we did not have any serious fighting we accomplished the entire pacification of a district the size of Ontario by doing a cakewalk through it with a chip on our shoulder, so to speak. The troops are now as hard as nails, and so are the horses that have not left their bones on the desert.

---

## 45  THE CAPTURE OF PRETORIA

*Le Soleil, Quebec*
*June 5, 1900* [translation]

It was barely nine o'clock this morning when the news of the capture of Pretoria by the British army arrived in Quebec on the wires of the Associated Press.

A few seconds later all the newspapers of the old capital announced the important news on their posters, and a little later, the joyful sound of our churchbells rhythmically proclaimed the happy event so feverishly expected by our entire population for the last few days.

Flags and decorations were at once put up on all public buildings and in all streets.

The whole good city of Quebec, the old French city, always loyal, exhibited in this spontaneous fashion its exuberant joy at the announcement of this great success for British arms.

For none can be in any doubt that the capture of Pretoria brings to a final end the bloody tragedy which has commanded the attention of the whole world for the past several months and which had as its stage the burning plains of Southern Africa.

Quebec rejoices because it is the end of a war dedicated to the principle of justice and protection of the rights of citizens ... Our brave men ... have played their part in defending the honor of the British flag under whose shelter we enjoy our rights as citizens and form a nation that has just caught the attention of the entire world.

## 46  THE DISLOYALTY OF HENRI BOURASSA

*The Citizen, Ottawa*
*June 8, 1900*

### THE MEMBERS HISSED BOURASSA'S DISLOYALTY

———

MEMBER FOR LABELLE INSULTS THE PATRIOTIC FEELING OF THE HOUSE BY MAKING PRO-BOER SPEECH AND BELITTLING ACHIEVEMENTS OF THE BRITISH ARMY

———

HISSES, GROANS GREET HIS REMARKS AND AT THEIR CONCLUSION MEMBERS RISE AND CHEER THE QUEEN—JOHN CHARLTON THROWS DOWN THE LIBERAL TRAITOR

Yesterday for the first time in its history, hisses were heard in the Canadian House of Commons, and these unusual signals of dissent were called forth by probably the first gratuitous expression of disloyalty ever uttered in the chamber. So long as the Boer advocate from Labelle confined his bombast to disquisitions drawn from pro-Boer pamphlets, and delivered upon pertinent occasions of debate, his offensiveness was treated with toleration due to inexperience and overweening conceit. But consideration for these failings of his changed into expressions of disgust and disapproval when yesterday the member for Labelle ... made a disloyal attack upon the British cause in South Africa and a studiously offensive reference to the achievements of the British army in which Canada's noble sons have participated so prominently ...

One salutory effect of this otherwise deplorable incident was the occasion it afforded for a general expression of loyal and patriotic feeling. No sooner had the member for Labelle resumed his seat, which he did amidst a renewed storm of dissent from all parts of the chamber, than Dr. Montague arose and suggested, as an antidote to the disloyalty which the house had been obliged to taste, "Three cheers for Her Majesty." The response was electrifying in its spontaneity and enthusiasm. Never were cheers more heartily given; certainly never was the national anthem that followed sung with greater gusto in parliament.

## A TERRIBLE ROW!

Sir Charles has a shocking Disagreement with the most Eminent Statesman of his acquaintance!

[Reproduced from J. W. Bengough: Cartoons of the Campaign 1900, *Toronto: The Poole Publishing Company, 1900.*]

## 47 A BOER MEETS A FRENCH CANADIAN

*The Globe, Toronto*
*August 13, 1900*

Dr. Fiset captured for a period by the Boers,
meets the brilliant Boer commando leader
General Christian de Wet.

Elandsfontein Junction, ten miles east of
Johannesburg, June 12—(In camp with the
Royal Canadian Regiment) ... A pleasant event occurred this evening—the return of Surgeon-Captain Fiset. I have
already told of his being left behind at
Heilbron and falling into the hands of the
Boers. He soon recovered, but was re-
tained by them for some days. Then
General Macdonald came along with his
Highland Brigade. Heilbron once more
changed hands and Captain Fiset was
free...
    Dr. Fiset was fairly well treated, and
Christian Dewet [*sic*] the Boer General,
who has several brilliant feats of arms to
his credit, was especially civil. They had a
talk of half an hour. At first the Boers were
amazed to find a Frenchman in the British uniform, and when they grasped the
fact that he was a French Canadian great
interest was shown. General Dewet in-
quired with the greatest interest about the
Canadian constitution and asked Captain
Fiset how the French were treated,
whether their language was allowed, and
on a variety of other points bearing upon
the relations of the races. Evidently Dewet
who is making a superb stand now, is looking ahead to a future co-operation between
two races.

## 48 FRENCH-CANADIAN DOMINATION

*The Globe, Toronto*
*November 9, 1900*

Ethnic Tensions in the federal election of
November 1900.

Although the election is over and the
incendiaries are deprived of their chief
reason for setting race against race, torch-
bearers of passion and race prejudice still
continue their vile work. *The News*
(Toronto) last night said:
    "In all its history Canada has not come
through an election that left so many reasons for apprehension as the contest
which closed yesterday. What the ultimate
result will be of Sir Wilfrid Laurier's
dividing the two races as he has done it
would require a prophet to tell, but it is an
intolerable condition for the English-
speaking Canadians to live under the
domination of the French ... We cannot
but regard the defeat of the Conservative
Party as a calamity to the people of Canada, inasmuch as it leaves in control of
the Government men who have proven to
be unfaithful to their trust. But it is
infinitely worse that the Government of
the day should hold power by reason of
the massing of one section of the community, speaking a foreign language and
holding ideals alien to the governing race
in the country."

## 49 THE DEATH OF QUEEN VICTORIA

*La Vérité, Quebec*
*January 26, 1901* [translation]

Her Majesty Alexandrina Victoria, Queen
of the United Kingdom of Great Britain
and Ireland, Empress of India, born in
London on May 24, 1819, has died in her
Osborne residence on the Isle of Wight,
on January 22, 1901 in her 82nd year.
    She always enjoyed the love and esteem
of her subjects and the respect of foreign
nations.
    Her reign—of almost 64 years—was the
longest in English history.
    During this period Great Britain consid-
erably expanded her Empire and increased
her prestige but often at the price of wars
that many could not approve of and
which the Sovereign herself must often
have deplored.
    It is said that the present South African
war greatly displeased her. It was even

hoped that she would abdicate rather than consent to it. But basely deceived by her ministers and bowed by age she seems to have done nothing to prevent it. It is a matter of keen regret to those who have genuine respect for royal authority. The disasters and humiliations suffered by England in the last fifteen months in Africa and the conviction that she had been misled by her ministers and some of her generals must have crushed her in sorrow and hastened the end of her days. Her long reign ended in tears and mourning.

God Alone Is Great.

## 50 THE BARBARIZING EFFECTS OF WAR

*The Weekly Sun, Toronto*
*January 30, 1901, p.1*

Here *The Weekly Sun* of Goldwin Smith denounces the barbarism of the British troops in the war in a way which was quite exceptional for the press of English Canada.

The London *Times*, as might be expected, scouts the idea of sending Sir Wilfrid Laurier out as mediator. To one of the parties no name could be less acceptable. It might be said more hateful. With the British the people of the South African Republics feel that at all events they had a quarrel; with Canadians they had none; and they demur to being sniped and having their houses burned, as they suspect, to gratify love of adventure or thirst for glory.

In South Africa it has come not only to the burning of farm-houses, but to the destruction of villages in which there can hardly fail to be aged men and women, sick persons, and children at the breast. An Australian after witnessing the burning of a Boer village says: "I looked on, telling myself that all this must be; that as things are we must war on the women to bring the men to subjection." Sir Charles Napier, the conqueror of Scinde, a fiery but chivalrous soldier, did not think that such things must be. On learning that vil- lages had been destroyed under his command, his words were: "What! Bri- tish troops destroying villages and leaving poor children and young children to perish! I can hardly believe this, but will take good care it never happens again under my command." He goes on to de- nounce the practice as "at variance with humanity and contrary to the usages of civilized war." Should the troops again be called upon to act, he orders that "war shall be made on men, not upon defence- less women and children, by destroying their habitations and leaving them to perish without shelter by the inclemencies of the winter." The Imperial Federation too will have entirely to eliminate the Dutch population of South Africa, which, after all, is the majority, if they mean to include that colony in the union.

## 51 LAURIER THE INTERNATIONAL STATESMAN

*Le Soleil, Quebec*
*March 23, 1901* [translation]

Laurier's international stature is stressed by *Le Soleil*. His speech on Bourassa's motion was widely acclaimed. The following extract is from a letter to Ernest Pacaud, editor, from an English journalist.

London was wild with enthusiasm over Sir Wilfrid Laurier's speech on the Bourassa motion. He is doing more to keep Canada to the front than any other public man has done because his speeches attract atten- tion to the Dominion not only in England but all over the continent. It is with pride that Canadians hear him spoken of from the street arab to the highest in the land. When his latest great address was pub- lished in all the papers here, there was a consensus of opinion as to its patriotic character, and the opinion was freely ex- pressed that the Canadian premier would likely have a say in the final settlement of the South African question. Canadians who have not been in this country since Sir Wilfrid's visit here can form no correct idea of the immense hold he has on the people of England.

---

# 52 AMERICAN PREENING UNWARRANTED

*The Province, Vancouver*
*April 23, 1901*

Those kind friends of the British Empire, the American papers, find great enjoyment in describing the prowess of Dewet [*sic*] and the consequent confusion of the British troops in South Africa. The work of quieting the new British colonies is admittedly slow, but notwithstanding much greater difficulties, the operations have been attended with much greater success than marked the campaign of the Americans in the Philippines. It took them about three years to capture Aguinaldo, but in South Africa there are half-a-dozen Aguinaldos each roaming about in a district in which the Philippines could be packed away and lost. The Filipinos against whom the Americans acted were in some part semi-savages quite uninstructed in the use of modern weapons many even being armed with bows and arrows. They have had no long lines of communications to guard and still they have 60,000 soldiers employed. Things have been very different in the Boer War, so that on the whole there is every reason to believe that Britain is doing a masterly job which will at last be completed properly. In the Philippines, on the other hand, it is notorious that no American is safe half a mile from a fortified post.

---

# 53 BOURASSA'S UNFOUNDED BUGBEAR

*Le Soleil, Quebec*
*October 30, 1901* [translation]

*Le Soleil* reacts strongly to "General" Henri Bourassa's latest speech.

General Bourassa: We are being asked what we think of Mr. Henri Bourassa's latest outburst. Good Heavens! To whom can we compare him if not to those hooligans who used to turn in false fire alarms to the despair of our good old fire chief Dorval, amusing themselves by forcing peaceful citizens to jump out of bed just for the pleasure of seeing them run to the window in their cotton nightcaps to look for the fire, when there wasn't a wisp of smoke.

Everyone knows the fable, especially its sad end, of the practical joker who shouted wolf, wolf and then laughed at the people who came rushing up. Mr Bourassa will end up by getting nabbed, just like all those who sound false alarms. The last time he shouted "Imperialism" every simple little fireman in Montreal came running...

The black peril of imperialism, which has become the favorite bee in Mr. Bourassa's bonnet is a scarecrow good enough for starlings. It scarcely alarms serious people but it is very useful to bring out the cheaper patriots. Grandson of Papineau, Mr. Henri Bourassa is being a little impudent, believing himself obliged by hereditary right to pose as leader on the barricades. It is a question of atavism, nothing more.

Alas, his example only serves to bring out once more one of our race's greatest inherent weaknesses, a national flaw which, let us quickly say, our compatriots are fully aware of and are working hard to correct. We refer to this need to snap and tear at each other that in the past has done so much damage to the French Canadian race. Mr. Bourassa would like to reintroduce this epidemic for which the cure has at last been found. His appeals to the old feelings of hatred for the English are not the real substance in his wordy and disorderly harangues: what he is really aiming at is the target of his old friend and protector Sir Wilfred Laurier. With what misused eloquence does he seek to tarnish the reputation of a statesman whose only crime has been to do honor to his race by the recognised skill with which he occupies the first position of responsibility in a multinational country. For what other purpose are these legends, these anecdotes and these insinuations that deliberately fall short of a categoric accusation, than to try to destroy Sir Wilfred Laurier in the opinion and esteem of his own compatriots? Czolgosz [President McKinley's assassin] hiding his murderous revolver in his handkerchief, only put into practice the hints of some agent provocateur, but it wasn't the latter who was electrocuted.

Mr. Bourassa poses in vain; he is neither Kaiser Wilhelm who has forgotten his encouraging letter to Kruger, nor even Tsar Nicholas who, it is reported, has just refused to mediate in favor of the Boers. Just why then does he want to enrol a handful of peaceful French Canadians under Dewet's [sic] and Botha's flag, when the biggest military nations of continental Europe have wisely withdrawn from the scene, lest they compromise themselves?

We distrust those posthumous patriots of 1837 whose legs were generally more agile than their tongues. Look at them as they then were: from the depths of their fits of Anglophobia they treat the English as Francophobes! The first to provoke trouble, they are the first to make excuses, they never said a word—these fanatics must be heard groaning of the fanaticism that they first began.

Sensible people understand much better what moral courage is all about. The real patriots are not those who loudly proclaim themselves to be such and who seek to uselessly compromise their race; they are rather those who work to raise its social and political prestige and to prepare it for the struggle in the arena of the arts, industry and commerce, the only real battlefield on this free soil of North America. We shall show that we are indeed of our own country and our own time if we refuse to let ourselves be distracted by discussion of imperial affairs.

This imperial federation which so frightens Mr. Bourassa, does he not know that it is a matter of little significance even in England? People talk about it more in one day in Canada than in a whole year over there. Rarely do the big London newspapers mention it unless to make fun of it, as Sir Charles Dilke has done in some powerful articles. Justin McCarthy has written the history of the whole Victorian era to our own days: a book like his would not leave anything out. Well, General Bourassa can leaf through its contents from first page to last and if he comes across a single mention of imperial federation we will present him with a brand new wooden sword.

## 54 THE ANTITHESIS BETWEEN WAR AND CHRISTIANITY

*The Globe, Toronto*
*December 10, 1901*

The speeches made by several professors of McMaster University after Professor Goldwin Smith's address on war show that there has been a good deal of uneasiness among conscientious men as to the manifestations of warlike spirit which have been made in this country in recent years. One remark made was that there had been a conflict in a good many hearts between the claims of patriotism and of Christian duty. To a certain extent such a conflict is inevitable. Christianity has for its basis the idea of the common brotherhood of man...

... War, even when necessary or justifiable, is deplorable, not a thing to be regarded as a means of pleasurable excitement.... The less glamor the better.

## 55 REASONS FOR THE SCARCITY OF FRENCH-CANADIAN OFFICERS

*Le Soleil, Quebec*
*December 23, 1901* [translation]

The Honorable Mr. Borden explains that there are no French Canadians among the officers of the Canadian Mounted Rifles because preference was given to those who had already served in Africa or in the Mounted Police and who had offered their services. French Canadians in this category are very few.

## 56 THE APOTHEOSIS OF THE CANADIAN SOLDIER

*The Star, Montreal*
*April 8, 1902*

The War and Canadian nationalism:
a Conservative view near the end of the war.

No name will come out of the South African War brighter than that of "the Canadian soldier."

Wherever he has been severely tried, he has acquitted himself not only with credit, but with brilliancy. From Paardeberg to Hart's River, he has shown the steadiness of the veteran,. linked with the splendid daring of the Light Brigade.

We Canadians who have stayed at home should feel no false modesty in proclaiming our pride in this. It is emphatically for us to say it.

We have not done the deed but we will profit by it. Our name will gain immensely in prestige throughout the empire and the world because these brothers of ours died fighting and victorious on the battle line. If they had flinched we would have suffered. But they met death with a superb courage, and we shall go out among the peoples of the world with a reputation for daring.

It might have been expected, to begin with, that "raw colonials" would not have stood fire. It will never be expected again. Our volunteers have established the reputation of the colonial soldier. There is not a military camp in Europe where we will not be ranked higher for the sacrifice of these men.

It is not only our privilege to boast this but our duty. We should make it clear to all coming generations that we appreciate to the full the work done by these young Canadians. The movements to mark their graves in South Africa and to erect fitting monuments to them here, are the natural expressions of a grateful people.

The gratitude is real enough and deep enough; and we must not be careless about the permanent expression of it.

## 57 RELATIONS BETWEEN BRITISH AND COLONIAL OFFICERS

*The Star, Montreal*
*August 9, 1902*

Lord Roberts has been under the necessity of issuing a memorandum calling upon British army officers to behave more decently towards their colonial confrères. The fact confirms numerous reports that were in circulation during the war, to the effect that a good deal of snobbishness had been exhibited by some of the curled darlings of the army toward colonial officers, who were their equals in military rank, and often their superiors in efficiency. ... Now to tell the plain truth the superiority of the aristocractic Briton over his colonial confrère, during the late war, was not nearly so obvious to the general public as it appeared to be to himself. Even men as capable of judging as Lord Roberts failed to recognize it. There is a widespread demand in England just now for army reform, and a very general impression that the greatest room for improvement is among the officers. Their courage and patriotism are not questioned but there is a feeling that as a class they attach too much importance to the professional side. Every instance of snobbery which comes to light will only tend to accentuate this feeling. That the majority of British officers are snobbish enough to treat their colonial confrères with rudeness we do not believe; but there seems to be enough of this class to injure the efficiency of the service, and Lord Roberts has done well to express his opinions on the subject.

## 58 A PRESCIENT VIEW OF SOUTH AFRICA'S FUTURE

*La Patrie, Montreal*
*May 10, 1902* [translation]

I do not know what the results will be of the official interviews now going on between Boer delegates and British army leaders. But during my stay in Africa I heard many times that the war was to end on the next day and I know of quite a few negotiations that came to nothing.

How will this latest one turn out? Will there be a truce, an armistice or even an apparent peace? We shall soon know. For my part I have many reasons for believing peace to be impossible, knowledge derived from hearing the heads of both sides state the conditions which each belligerent will demand before ending hostilities. Whatever happens, even if by chance a peace treaty is officially concluded between Mr. Shalk-Burger and Lord Kitchener, it will be an artificial peace, purely diplomatic and, as it were, for decoration only.

I really believe that the struggle between the English and Dutch elements in South Africa cannot end. It is always dangerous to pose as a prophet, even on the other side of the world from one's own country. But perhaps, without excessive boldness, I can get beyond a factual narration to attempt an explanation of the deeper causes of the war and the real reasons for its having gone on so long.

The deeper causes are the moral ones. It is more than a dispute between neighbors over borders; more even than an outburst of good or evil passions about gold buried in the earth; it is a conflict of two races all the more irreconcilable since both are driven by a mystical force.

The mystique of the Boers is well known. Since Mr. Kruger came to Europe he has on several occasions displayed his quite Biblical piety. But many people suppose that the old President is an exception. Nothing of the kind. President Kruger thinks and talks like all his race. All Boers, young and old have this same confidence in God and calm assurance in their faith. One July evening in Pretoria when British communiqués were announcing the final defeat of Boer troops I went into the old church around which the town grew up. The winter twilight straggled in through the door and I heard the slow chant of hymns.

Not one complaint, not even a word of sorrow. Those brave people were giving thanks to God. "We thank the Lord," one of them told me, "for not having abandoned us and we beg him to continue his favors to us for our trials may last a long time yet." That day I really felt the spirit of this people and realised that the war was only just beginning. Since then, everything that I have seen and learned of the Boers only confirms my first conclusion. Their resistance, their heroic resistance, their resignation in defeat, their magnanimity in victory have all to be seen in this light. The Boers are convinced that they are to resume in the vast African countryside the biblical life of the Old Testament and that they have been singled out by God for a mysterious destiny.

But in the face of this lofty, calm, patriarchal mystique, more or less invincible, there is an English mystique, less known but no less stubborn. Of course the British understand nothing of the Boer mystique, the Boers and their friends nothing of the British. It is the function of overheated passions to blind men to one another.

The British mystique is undeniable. It has not the peaceful and simple loftiness of the Boer feeling. It has something lofty and frantic about it, it is bitter, yet ardent, muddied by much earthly greed, dangerous, fierce, even hateful; all the same it is not without grandeur and its power is formidable. It is simultaneously national, martial and religious. It is a lot like the mystique of Republican Rome and Mohammed's Arabs. Like Virgil's hero [Aeneas] marvelling over the exploits of Marcellus, the British mystique willingly proclaims:

Tu regere imperio populos,
Romane, memento
[Remember, O Roman, to rule the world with your power]

The belief that England has a divine mission and that she is called to civilize the rest of the world might seem to us in France an odd play of the politicians or a bluff concealing the country's colonial expansion. That would be to judge this people superficially. This strange faith is sincere. And although often hidden it is fully evident if one looks hard enough.

"Possibly we are doing some harm at the

moment," a young major from Senior Intelligence told me, "but it is for the good of the world, and our destiny must be fulfilled even at the price of a little bloodshed." I came across this same feeling in soldiers' tents as in bureaucratic offices; it swelled the voices of religious ministers and on the eve of victory it caught up the whole army in its frenzy.

"Rule Britannia." This is not the shout of conquering vengeance, it is rather an avowal of mystical faith. And by a singular coincidence, this week, on the very day Mr. Henri des Houx reported in *Le Matin* Kruger's famous words: "God has led us up to now by the right hand" the great English novelist Rider Haggard, replying to a question from Mr. Ludovic Naudeau in *Le Journal* on southern Africa wrote: "That country will be one of the Imperial stars placed by destiny before Great Britain to lighten her path towards her mysterious and ineluctable goal..."

God has taken us by the hand
Mysterious, ineluctable goal!

We have here the two formulas of two mystiques in conflict. Which of the two is the stronger? It would take a bold man to measure them. War, long threatening, burst out three years ago. To all the other pretexts for quarrel there was added the feverish greed of gold-seekers. No concession was morally possible from the Boers and the British would consent to none. The moral causes being equally mysterious and profound, nothing can be done save to await the conflict's outcome and see which of the two armies can hold out the longest.

In the present state of things, barring any unforeseen event in world history, there is no reason why one of the two races should be finally conquered by the other.

At first glance it would seem that the British have great material advantages. They can reinforce their troops indefinitely, they control all means of transport, all harbors are open to their fleets, they hold the railroads, they can supply themselves with foodstuffs from all over the world. It might therefore be concluded that with time, money and patience, they must little by little fatally undermine the independence, strength and even the existence of the Dutch race.

So it would seem. In reality the situation of the British in South Africa is materially worse off than that of the Boers. Their new recruits are more and more inferior. Officers without experience, undisciplined mercenaries, an endlessly improvised army. And these hundreds of thousands of men literally melt away to nothing in the immense veldt. For every twelve men only one is a fighting man. All the rest are bogged down from Capetown to Fort Komati, from Durban to Mafeking, in guarding cities, camps, rivers, railways and blockhouses in a space as large as Southern Europe. And they are all obliged to be ever on the alert even around cities where danger is never foreseen. To this must be added the vagaries of climate, heat, drought, freezing temperatures at night, torrential downpours of rain and the frightful misery of epidemics.

The Boer soldiers on the other hand, from first to last, are tested fighters, used to fatigue, who move easily through their own country. No cities, no bridges, no roads to guard, no worries about complex administration. Still more, while the English spend day and night in constant watch, the Boers rest when they want to and control whole districts where they can enjoy as complete a security as the inhabitants of Ploërmel or Beaucaire.

Thus with ten thousand men—and there is no point inflating the number—the Boer army can hold in check one hundred, two hundred thousand invaders. Far from having to seek recruits, Boer generals have a reserve of new fighters who come to enrol. This is the way it is in far off districts and in the Cape Colony itself. And all losses are at once made up.

As for leaders, they are constantly coming forward as the war progresses. Around Botha, De Wet, Delarey there are men unknown to us who from one day to the next can replace them and accomplish the same deeds. The strength for this is in the people themselves.

On the one side then an invading army endlessly building itself up, but whose might is very limited. On the other a resistance army constantly renewing itself. On both sides, an equal stubborness. This war may last a long time.

Nevertheless, sooner or later, it will have to end. If I were to bet on one of the two races, it would be without hesitation on the Dutch. It inevitably will win the upper hand in Southern Africa. Here and now England can renounce the vast Dominion she had dreamed about and which was possible before the Jamieson Raid. Nothing which will happen in the history of the world can take anything from the Dutch of the Cape. The British, on the other hand, are putting up their maximum effort right now against the Boers. Were a European cataclysm to intervene or merely, for England, a forced diversion, it would be for her so much wasted effort in Africa.

But let us say that nothing intervenes and that England finally achieves her peace. Reconciliation between the races is from now on impossible. Hatreds will remain dormant, ready to flare up, and a handful of men will be unable to police a country where one hundred thousand soldiers were powerless.

Goldseekers' greed and the arrogance of new settlers will provoke endless quarrels, and it will all begin again. The Boer race will not be wiped out, it stretches from the Cape to the Limpopo and sober, patient and fertile it will regain its strength with every passing day.

And then Southern Africa, beyond the sea coast, offers no future for British settlement. It's only a vast desert fit for a pastoral life. The rivers there are uncontrollable and any thought of cultivation is pure fantasy. There is wealth underground. But the mines will quickly be exhausted. 10 years, 20 years, even 50 years and the smokestacks of abandoned mines will have crumbled on to the veldt where flocks of sheep will graze. Every English and foreign element will abandon this now sterile land. And the Boers will begin again their free life in the open air. They will once again become the undisputed masters of Southern Africa, even if a few businesses remain in British hands.

And travellers a century from now who cross those silent sun-lit fields, where here and there flourishes a lonely farm will wonder what fit of madness possessed a people who count Shakespeare, Milton, Bacon and Gladstone in their number, to provoke so much hatred, spill so much blood, spend so much money and disturb the conscience of the world for the sake of a dream and for rule over a wasteland.

Jean Carrere

---

## 59  A BOER POEM

*Le Soleil, Quebec*
*June 7, 1902* [translation]

A corner of Africa. It has no rival
For its groves, its rocks, its shores, its soil
For its flocks and its fields. Transvaal . . .
In its mourning countryside, along a
    pretty valley
Its soil worn away by grey tracks,
Their hair whipped by the spring breezes
Two Boers, a youth and an old man, riding,
The youth was surprised at the holes in the
    ground
"War, my child, long and bitter war—there
    our
Heroes sleep," said the old man with pride.
He gazed steadily at the countless trenches
Suddenly he clasped his rough, big hands
And with a sob cried out: "There lies
    freedom."

---

## 60  BRITISH MAGNANIMITY

*The Canadian Churchman, Toronto*
*June 12, 1902*

In spite of the news reports many Canadians held a very idealistic view of Britain's efforts right through the Boer War.

The war was conducted with unparalleled humanity, and new precedents have been established in this respect which will do much to mitigate the horrors of war in the future . . . The termination of this unhappy war will bring, not only relief but lasting benefits to the loyalists of South Africa, for the maintenance of whose rights the war was chiefly waged, to the Kaffirs and black races of Africa at large, and though last, not least, to our brave but misguided foe, who under British sovereignty will enjoy greater liberty, and make greater progress commercially and otherwise than was possible under the antiquated and unprogressive policy and methods of the late Dutch Republics. The terms of peace, so far as are known at present, are not only just but magnanimous and are assented to by all parties in the state, and reflect infinite credit on the Government, and especially on Mr. Chamberlain, Mr. Milner, and Lord Kitchener.

## 61 FRENCH CANADA MUST BE CONVERTED TO PROTESTANTISM

*The Spectator, Hamilton*
*June 17, 1902*

Part of the Report of the General Assembly of the Presbyterian Church of Canada held at Toronto.

One delegate Rev. George C. Pidgeon noted that the present state of the province of Quebec was a menace to the peace and security of Canada. The Real Question, etc. had started there.

Rev. J. E. Duclos took the most pronounced view on the question, holding that only the spread of the gospel as Protestants hold it, throughout Quebec could save Canada from the most serious consequences, and make the French Canadian people really loyal to the British Crown. A religious conquest (not one of gun powder) of Quebec was necessary to the maintenance of Protestant supremacy and to generate a new national spirit. The power of Quebec was now felt from ocean to ocean and he feared the intrigues and the machinations of Rome in the government because of this.

# Section IV

## The Colonial Conference of 1902 And Its Aftermath

# 1 CANADA AND IMPERIAL DEFENCE

*The Star, Montreal*
*January 20, 1898*

Sir Richard Cartwright has been declaring our loyalty in Toronto, and Sir Michael Hicks-Beach has been suggesting that we prove it by contributing something to naval defences. Probably nothing would be more popular in Canada than the building and manning of a Canadian battleship to be placed at the disposal of the British Government. Other methods of dropping the Canadian mite into the Imperial box may be proposed which will be more in keeping with our resources and needs and perhaps worthier of our position in the Empire; but it is doubtful if any would be more spectacularly popular.

Two things certainly might be done very easily. A recruiting station for a Canadian regiment could be established in the Dominion, and a training ship where Canadian youths bitten with a desire to serve in the navy might be initiated, could be anchored at one of our ports. This would foster a personal interest among our people in Imperial campaigns all over the world, and tend to increase the solidarity of the British nation whose boundaries include Australia and Devonshire, Dawson City and London Town. A family who had a son fighting on the frontiers of India or sailing with a ship in the China sea, would realize very vividly that they belong to the people which is leading in the government of the planet.

---

# 2 IMPERIAL DEFENCE: THE FEAR OF EXTERNAL CONTROL

*The Globe, Toronto*
*May 3, 1899*

General Hutton, the imperial officer who commanded the Canadian militia, was an outspoken advocate of imperial military links. His determination to press for extensive reform of the militia raised constitutional questions as to whether he was responsible to London or Ottawa, questions which influenced the outcome of the 1902 Colonial Conference.

Speaking at the recent meeting of the Officers' Association of the Militia, Major-General Hutton made a noteworthy statement as to his footing in this country. *The Canadian Military Gazette* thus reports him:—

> "There is one point upon which, with your permission, I should like to say one word. It is this: In some of the columns of the Canadian press I see it stated that I came to Canada with a mission as regards the military future of this country. This statement is correct, absolutely correct. My mission was this: I was told most clearly by the Secretary of State for the Colonies and the Secretary of State for War before leaving London: 'Go to Canada and do your utmost to improve their militia, and advise the Government as to the necessary requirements for the defence system of Canada.' This is, and has been, my aim and object since my arrival, and it will be my privilege and my duty, during the whole period of my command to follow these instructions. I should, however, like to add that I, and I alone, am responsible for the means that I have adopted and for the advice that I have conceived it my duty to tender to the Minister of Militia and Defence and to the Canadian Government. I accept all the responsibility, and am prepared to render an account of my acts and of my recommendations."

... It appears that Mr. Chamberlain and Lord Lansdowne have given to Major-General Hutton a mission which has been entrusted to no previous General Officer Commanding the Militia. It would follow that the Major-General is responsible to the two British Ministers for the due discharge of this mission. But by our Militia Act he is responsible to the Canadian Minister of Militia and Defence, and to him alone, saving the general duty he owes to his official superiors in the army, by whom he is lent to Canada to be charged with 'the military command and discipline of the militia' ... In order to induce Canada to bring her armed strength up to the point of efficiency which prevails elsewhere in the empire they have resorted to the method of charging, apparently by word of mouth, an officer who is usually simply the subordinate of the Canadian Minister of Militia and Defence with an additional mission practically involving the desired reorganization.

That the Imperial Statesman of such acknowledged regard for the value and importance of Greater Britain should feel impelled to charge the General Officer Commanding our Militia with such a mission can hardly prove altogether agreeable to Canadians...

The interesting point is that this important development in Canadian affairs should be taken upon the initiative of two gentlemen who hold their official positions at the pleasure of British electors. Our autonomy is so large that we are very seldom reminded of the curious gap which exists in the chain of responsibility for Governmental acts ... A certain line of action is indicated to us by Imperial statesmen as desirable and we are requested to adopt it. Considering all the circumstances, the appeal from the mother country, which has been so generous a protector and which safeguards our interests at such vast expense, is irresistible. But there is a natural tendency to balk at the appearance of external control, and this incident, delicately as the home authorities have managed their request, brings forcibly before us the fact of the incompleteness which yet attends our imperial organization. Only occasionally does the course of events drag this incompleteness into public notice, but it exists none the less. There lies the significant feature of the incident.

# 3  DOES CANADA NEED NAVAL DEFENCE?

*The Weekly Sun, Toronto*
*January 9, 1901*

Great Britain is still, in our fancy, an insular power, secure in her bulwark of sea and needing no towers along the steep. While she was really such, she might be content with a strong yet not extravagant navy and a standing army on a moderate scale. Now that she has expanded, or, to speak more truly, scattered herself over all the quarters of the globe, nothing less will suffice for her security than the complete command of all the seas. For this a navy of overwhelming magnitude is required. But the other nations naturally object to the extinction of their maritime independence, and seek to restore the freedom of the seas. They vie with Great Britain in the construction of battleships, and upon every (increase) of their navies there is a cry for an increase of hers. The other day, an addition to her navy having been announced, announcements of additions to the French and German navies at once followed. Into this mad race of naval expenditure Canada, if a party among us has its way, will be drawn. It is said, and sounds reasonable, that we ought to contribute to our naval defence. But were it not for the challenge continually thrown out to the world by Imperialist ambition, we should need no naval defence at all. Our only possible assailant is the United States, a war with which, considering the relations, commercial and general, between the two communities, has been truly said to be about as likely as collision with another planet. Nor, if we were at war with the United States, could an Imperial navy protect us. An American flottila, or even a single vessel, on Lake Superior, where no Imperial fleet could reach it, would raid the Pacific Railway and cut our Dominion in two. But we need not talk about a hateful contingency which, unless some transcendent act of folly is committed, will never occur.

## 4 LAURIER WILL PROTECT CANADIAN AUTONOMY

*La Patrie, Montreal*
*March 14, 1902* [translation in the
Montreal *Star,* March 15, 1902]

It is with profound satisfaction that the whole country will read the reply [to Britain's invitation to discuss political relations within the Empire at the forthcoming Colonial Conference] of the Laurier Government. Sir Wilfrid Laurier and his colleagues inform Mr. Chamberlain that they neither intend to change such present political relations nor to modify them, that there can be no question of establishing a system of defence applicable to the whole empire, and that, in truth, there will be nothing else to debate at the London Conference than the problem of commercial relations within the empire. The reply of the government is categorical. It indicates in an irresistible manner that the Laurier ministry does not intend to sacrifice, nor to allow the sacrifice of the political liberties which our fathers conquered, nor of the national sovereignty, whose price we thoroughly appreciate. It will hermetically seal the mouth of the political charlatans who for months and months have endeavoured to poison the opinion of the people by spreading everywhere the rumour that Sir Wilfrid Laurier is to deliver us bound hand and foot to devouring imperialism, to sell to Mr. Chamberlain our rights and our constitution.

## 5 STRONG SUPPORT FOR IMPERIAL DEFENCE

*The Mail and Empire, Toronto*
*March 14, 1902*

Many hoped that the Boer War would lead to a military federation of the empire. When the subject was raised in connection with the invitations to the Colonial Conference of 1902, Laurier rejected the proposal and many English Canadians were unhappy.

Widely different are the views taken of the Ottawa deliverance on the question of Imperial defence. In England there is a feeling of keen disappointment that Canada should, through its premier, have treated the matter in a way that is lukewarm, if not worse. By the enemies of imperialism everywhere Sir Wilfrid Laurier is lauded for his attitude. Mr. Labouchere hails Canada as the opponent of naval and military cooperation in the defence of the empire. *La Patrie* exults in the death-knell of Imperial defence sounded, as it believes, by Sir Wilfrid Laurier. There can be no doubt that the correspondence recently published justifies these critics in the opinions they have formed of the attitude of the premier, but it is premature for them to conclude that he represents the matured judgement of Canada. ... Imperial defence is not a matter that can be flippantly thrust aside by shallow objection. It is as essential to us as it is to any part of the empire, and it is as warmly supported by the loyal people here as by Britons anywhere. Sir Wilfrid has not heard the last of this matter. If he is wise he will reconsider this deliverance, provided he has considered it at all, and will voice the well-known sentiments of Canada at the forthcoming conference. If he is in doubt Parliament should put him right and keep him there.

## 6 CANADA AND IMPERIAL TRADE

*The Province, Vancouver*
*March 18, 1902*

The Liberal press saw Laurier and Chamberlain working closely together to achieve imperial economic goals.

... The Colonial Secretary, Mr. Joseph Chamberlain, who is ardently in sympathy with the views entertained by Sir Wilfrid Laurier and other colonial premiers, has practically stated that the whole question of Imperial trade relations will be open for discussion, and he has himself indicated his belief that a preference on colonial goods in the English market must be the result of the closer business dealings between Great Britain and her colonies. It is this aim that the Canadian premier has been advocating; this result which he has been striving for since his advent to power in this country; and every year has seen his views meet a quicker and larger response on the part of leaders of public opinion in England.

# 7 UNITY BEFORE PROFITS

*The Globe, Toronto*
*April 19, 1902*

Laurier is advised by the *Globe* not to wrangle for concessions from Britain at the Colonial Conference of 1902 in London.

By all means let us have a preferential tariff if we can get it without wrangling and acrimony, but let us regard it rather as the apex than as the base of that essential unity of the empire which already exists in the mind and will of the free peoples under the British flag and which is being every day exemplified by the loftiest patriotism and the most generous devotion.

# 8 AN IMPERIAL COURT OF APPEAL: NEW THREAT TO CANADIAN AUTONOMY?

*The Canadian Magazine, Toronto*
*June 1900*

W. Sandford Evans sees the proposed new Imperial Court of Appeal as resulting in the British Parliament, rather than the Crown, becoming the focal point of the Empire.

On May 14, Mr Chamberlain introduced into the Imperial House of Commons "The Commonwealth of Australia Constitutions Act" and the bill was read a first time. This bill was first drafted at the famous Sydney convention of 1891, and it has been redrafted at subsequent conven-

tions. It was twice submitted to a referendum and in its present form was sanctioned by a large majority in the Colonies applying for federation ... The British Government had wanted it changed in some respects ... Objection centred around Clause 74. This clause prohibited any appeal from the High Court of Australia to the Queen-in-Council, in any matter involving the interpretation of the new constitution...

The difference of opinion on the question of appeal gave an opportunity to the Imperial Government to propose the formation of an Imperial Court of Appeal for the whole Empire. Appeals from the British Isles now go to a committee of the House of Lords, while appeals from other portions of the Empire go to the Judicial Committee of the Privy Council. The membership of these committees is much the same, but the bodies are distinct. The Government proposes to make one body of them, adding to the present membership a representative of Canada, South Africa, Australia and India. The colonial representatives would be made members of the Privy Council and life Peers, although their terms of office as judges would be seven years. The new Imperial Court of Appeal would be a committee of the House of Lords, the judicial functions of the Privy Council disappearing. This scheme has the one great recommendation of unifying the final interpretation of law for the whole Empire. There are other evident advantages from the Imperial standpoint. But may there not also be disadvantages? In some of its aspects the matter is too technical ... But should we not carefully watch anything which introduces a change, even in form, from the British Crown as the centre of the Empire to one of the Houses of Parliament? The English Liberals see objections from their point of view, and all that can here be done is to state the conviction that this is a matter Canadians should discuss.

# 9 THE LINE OF LEAST RESISTANCE

*The Globe, Toronto*
*June 9, 1902*

Some curious speculations are afloat in regard to the meeting of the colonial Premiers in London during the coronation ceremonies. One writer goes so far as to suggest that it may bring about a crisis in British politics, and be immediately followed by a general election. The theory appears to be that the colonies will "insist" upon a preference in the British markets, and that this will be bitterly opposed by one of the great British parties, and by the masses of Great Britain, who are deeply attached to free trade, and would resent any policy which meant dear bread.

It would be strange, indeed, if a meeting called for the purpose of promoting unity should bring about dissension and even endanger the integrity of the empire, and we are sure that the view is needlessly gloomy. The colonies have no intention of "insisting" on preferential trade as a right, or of pressing it if they find it opposed by the masses of the British people. Preferential trade would have absolutely no standing unless it benefited the people of the United Kingdom as well as those of the colonies. And if the people of the United Kingdom are resolutely opposed to it, there is an end of it. The taxpayers of Great Britain have the matter in their own hands. We cannot tax them, and there is something almost comical in the suggestion that the old country should follow the example of the Americans a hundred and twenty-five years ago, and break away from the tyrannical colonies that are trying to oppress them with new taxes.

However, there is a serious element in all this. Strong party feelings and strong class feelings will undoubtedly be aroused by the attempt to restore protection in Great Britain. Is it wise for the colonies to take sides on such a question, and especially to take sides in such a way as will lead to the suspicion that they are seeking to promote their own interests under cover of Imperialism? How should we relish the interference of the people of the United Kingdom in our party politics? Would it tend to unify the empire, or the reverse? We suppose that in ordinary times the Liberal party in Great Britain is just about as numerous as the Conservative party. What sort of Imperial programme is it that tends to alienate one-half of the people of the old country? Much is said to-day about the old policy of indifference to the colonies. We have passed, it is said, to a happier order of things. But it would be worse than indifference if half or more of the British people should come to entertain an actual dislike for the colonies as allies of one political party or the other.

Time will show that Sir Wilfrid Laurier was right when he refused to demand the imposition of British taxes for the benefit of Canada. His Government took a step which really increased Imperial trade and promoted unity and good feeling—the reduction of the duties on British imports. It pleased British Conservatives and Liberals alike, the rich and the poor, protectionists and free traders; and it unquestionably led to an increased demand for Canadian products in Great Britain. Since then the British Government has imposed a duty on wheat and other grains and flour, which is declared to be for revenue purpose, but which is also said to be a leverage for some preferential trade plan. If that duty is removed in favor of the colonies, that will be some relief to the British consumer, and possibly some benefit to the Canadian farmer. But we do not believe the farmer wants to be placed in the position of begging or demanding any British tariff legislation whatever.

Some undesirable results may follow from the attempt to drive the Imperial horse too hard. Take the question of defence. Everything was going well before the attempt was made to strike a balance sheet, and say just what the colonies owe to Great Britain and what they ought to pay. Of course, this at once puts both parties into a bargaining frame of mind, and it is seen that there are items on both sides of the account. Why not have left events to march in the old way? The colonies were steadily progressing toward complete self-reliance in this matter, and had even rendered substantial aid to the mother country. Everybody was satisfied. Now a vote has been taken at a meeting of business men in which there is at least an appearance of division. So it was in the case of preferential trade. Our voluntary preferences were generally satisfactory, and, we believe, were as beneficial to Canada as to Great Britain. Then the parchment and the pens and ink and sealing wax were got out and an attempt was made to frame a scheme and obtain "equivalents," and have everything down in black and white. At once dissension and suspicion began. We know that this is a strenuous age, and that laissez-faire is a forbidden phrase. But there is some wisdom, after all, in the saying that the American colonies were lost by a Minister insisting on reading the American despatches. At all events, when legislation or government action is invoked, it should be on lines of least resistance; and in regard to some of these Imperial matters it looks as if the line of greatest resistance had been chosen, with the best intentions no doubt.

Without attempting to lay down any hard and fast scheme, the lines of co-operation between the United Kingdom and the colonies are not difficult to indicate. Underlying all is the feeling of good-will; and we must take care that this means good-will not merely between governing classes, rich and influential people, but between the masses of Great Britain and the masses here. Then, our preferential tariff is a measure of the right kind, and might be followed by the exemption of colonial products from the British tariff on grain, if that is to be continued. As to defence, we now assume the duty of our own land protection, and in due time a plan may be developed for coast and sea defence, which will enable us to relieve the taxpayer at home. But at present we think the most promising line of co-operation is that of transportation. If there is to be a shifting of shipping interests across the Atlantic, why should it not be to Canada, building up Canadian ports, and having Canadian farm products carried in British ships? At present our exports to Great Britain may not cut a great figure beside those of the United States, but they are proportionately increasing every year. There is a continually increasing surplus of that and other foods. At the same time the immigration that is pouring into the United States is of food-consumers rather than of food-producers. It is reasonable to suppose that there will be a great increase in the trade that finds its outlet by the St. Lawrence and the ports of the Maritime Provinces. This seems to indicate the most practical and useful form of co-operation between the United Kingdom and Canada. To convert the British Empire into a customs union like the United States is an attractive idea; but it arouses the opposition of free traders in England and of protectionists in Canada. No class of the community can reasonably object to the improvement of communication and transportation, which will increase the profits of trade without burdening the consumer or disturbing established industries.

---

## 10  A BLUEPRINT FOR CANADA

*The Globe, Toronto*
*June 18, 1902*

The *Globe* outlines the imperial program
Canada should adopt at the
Colonial Conference.

### CANADA AND THE EMPIRE

(1) Canada will rejoice to receive a preference for her products in the British markets, if without manifest coercion from the colonies that becomes the accepted policy of Great Britain.

(2) But with all our great natural wealth and potential industrial development, we cannot afford to clamor for doles from the mother country, and we doubt if true Imperial unity can be promoted by any policy which threatens to make the masses of Britain hostile to the outlying British kingdoms.

(3) We cannot afford to enter into an alliance with any British political party, nor

demand favors at Westminster which many leading British statesmen are certain to denounce as undue concessions to the colonies.

(4) An Imperial preferential tariff can be safely approached only upon the lines of remissions of taxation by Great Britain in favor of the colonies and remissions of taxation by the colonies in favor of Great Britain.

(5) Canada sympathizes with Mr. Chamberlain's vision of absolute free trade within the empire, but recognizes that for the present many of her industries cannot be exposed to the unobstructed sweep of British competition, and that we cannot conveniently raise by any system of direct taxation the millions of revenue that must be lost by the free admission of British goods.

(6) The natural desire of Great Britain is to manufacture for the colonies. The natural desire of the colonies is to develop home industries and to support a large industrial population. In this view the new Australian Commonwealth has adopted a protectionist tariff. In this view protectionists in Canada contend that the reduction of 33 1/3 per cent in favor of British goods has greatly prejudiced important Canadian industries.

(7) Mr. Chamberlain told Sir Wilfrid Laurier in 1897 that except upon the basis of free trade within the empire he would not touch preferential trade with a pair of tongs. This is still, so far as we know, the position of the Colonial Secretary, Sir Michael Hicks-Beach, the Duke of Devonshire, and Lord Salisbury. The Liberal leaders at home are unanimously opposed to a tax on food. Colonial protectionists and Imperialists make a tax on grain and food products the essential feature of their demand. We thus have, as Mr. Chamberlain has said, a proposition from the colonies which Great Britain cannot accept, and a proposition from Great Britain which the colonies cannot accept.

(8) Canadian Conservatives and many Imperialists persistently ignore the British demand for the complete abolition of taxes on British goods as the first and prime condition of a preferential tariff. If Canada accepted Imperial free trade, many of the men who now demand a preference in Britain would unite to punish the Government which accepted the essential conditions of the compact. In the meantime, so far as Canada is concerned, the existing preference in the Canadian tariff in favor of British goods is a fair equivalent for the remission in our favor of the new British revenue duties on corn.

(9) The British free trader and the Canadian protectionist approach the question of preferential tariff from wholly different standpoints. The British free trader argues that free trade would be good for Canada. The Canadian protectionist argues that protection would be good for Great Britain. The industries of Canada have been established upon a protectionist basis. The industries of Great Britain have been established upon a free trade basis. Free trade within the empire and protection against the rest of the world would involve a grave disturbance of industrial conditions in both countries, and greatly imperil many important industries.

(10) Since the Liberal Government took office at Ottawa six years ago we have introduced Imperial penny postage, contributed heavily to the Pacific cable, maintained a Canadian garrison in place of the British garrison at Halifax, contributed generously in men and money to the cause of the empire in South Africa, greatly increased our expenditures for defence at home and reduced by one-third the tariff on imports from Great Britain, and in return we have failed even to secure relief from the British restrictions upon the importation of Canadian cattle, or in any way to obtain better treatment in the British market than our competitors in the United States receive.

(11) It must always be difficult to strike a balance between trade and defence, but at least the heavily burdened British ratepayer should not be taxed for the defence of Canada. We are a young, rich and prosperous country, and should frankly meet all legitimate obligations on this account. We should relieve Great Britain of all expenditures of a military character in Canada. But, as the British taxpayer is not required to bear the enormous cost of developing the

great area of virgin territory which Canada possesses, so the Canadian taxpayer should not be required to bear in the same ratio as the European taxpayer the cost of militarism in the old world. Each country has its advantages and disadvantages of location. We must develop trade. The old world protects trade. In this protection the Canadian producer has no advantage or privilege which is not equally extended to the producer of the United States.

(12) The old world spends its millions on militarism. The new world spends its millions on settlement and development. Canada should not be required to bear the double burden and meet alike the cost of militarism in Europe and the cost of development in America. Each, we repeat, is entitled to its advantages as each must accept the disadvantages of its natural position and surroundings. It is unfair that Canada should be taxed for the support of the military armaments of Europe, and just as unfair that the heavily burdened British Islands should be taxed for the defence of Canada. This should be the permanent condition, as each should exhaust its resources for the other in case its integrity were assailed by any hostile combination.

(13) In transportation a basis of common action, without friction or complications exists. Great Britain needs the food products of Canada. Canada needs the British market. Every improvement in the means of transportation benefits alike the Canadian producer and the British consumer. In proportion as we cheapen the cost of transportation from the west to the seaboard, we guarantee better prices to the western farmer, and in proportion as we cheapen the means of carriage across the ocean we lower the cost to the British population of their food supply, whether imported from the colonies or from foreign countries.

(14) The most luminous chapter in the history of Canada is that which records the struggle for responsible government. The most lamentable chapter in the history of Britain is that which records the attempt of an arrogant King and obsequious Ministers to impose taxation without representation upon the American colonies. The extension of colonial self-government is synchronous with the growth of the Imperial spirit and the consolidation of the British Kingdoms. We may not predict what shall be the final outcome of this orderly evolution, nor risk dissension and disunion by premature attempts at organic union, which may limit the freedom of thé colonies and perhaps divide the people of Britain into colonial and anti-colonial factions.

(15) The sovereignty alike of the Imperial and the colonial Parliaments must be preserved. In popular sovereignty is the supreme efficacy of British institutions. How can we bind the colonies in advance to participation in all British wars; how bind Great Britain to inevitable sanction of all demands of her outlying kingdoms? These issues must be determined as they arise. Our aid will be none the less generous because it is voluntary. Our Imperial patriotism will be none the less intense and abounding because it is free of all taint of Imperial coercion. In the free action of all parts of the empire lies the best guarantee of harmonious and effective co-operation and the enduring stability of British institutions the world over.

---

## 11  THE COLONIAL CONFERENCE MEETS IN SECRET

*The Globe, Toronto*
*July 7, 1902*

The lips of the colonial Premiers are sealed while the Imperial conference is in secret session, and they content themselves with amiable platitudes when forced into after-dinner oratory. Sir Wilfrid Laurier, warned by the publication of an interview in New York, which he repudiates from beginning to end, tells me that he cannot discuss any question connected with the work of the conference. There is little faith among either the colonial Premiers or the British Imperialists that any results of great importance will be accomplished, either political or fiscal. Something may be done toward bringing about the co-operation of the mother country and the colonies in protecting maritime interests by liberal mail subsidies, but the preferential treatment is regarded by the English press as impracticable at present.

---

## 12 THE COLONIAL CONFERENCE AND SUBSIDIZED STEAMSHIPS

*The Globe, Toronto*
*July 18, 1902*

### THE FAST MAIL LINE

-----

### NEGOTIATIONS SAID TO BE IN ACTIVE PROGRESS

-----

Probable Attempt to Induce Britain to Increase the Subsidy She Has Already Pledged—Sir Wilfrid Laurier to Visit France.

-----

London, July 17. —It is evident from last night's speeches at the Canada Club dinner that Mr. Chamberlain's conference has made no substantial progress as yet towards a definite scheme of defence or the preferential tariff agreements. The chief result so far has been to discover how many different views are held, though the fraternal spirit is most marked. The preliminary of the fast mail line negotiations between the Canadian Ministers and Sir Christopher Furness and the Elder-Dempsters are still proceeding. The next step apparently will be to endeavor to induce Mr. Chamberlain to increase the British subsidy, which is now pledged at £75,000 against Canada's £150,000. That, however, must await Mr. Chamberlain's resumption of business. The general idea at present seems to be that a gigantic company will be floated here to construct a fast passenger service to Cape Breton with three new 22-knot steamers, costing one million pounds sterling each, the company also to buy the Furness and Elder-Dempster fleet for a cargo service to the St. Lawrence. It is hoped to induce the Australian Premiers to combine with Canada to improve the Vancouver-Australian fleet as a link in the fast mail service, and to bring London and Sydney within 25 days of each other.

## 13 THE RESULTS OF THE CONFERENCE

*The Globe, Toronto*
*August 13, 1902*

London, Aug. 12—While the results of the Colonial Conference, which ended yesterday, are generally considered satisfactory as far as they go, it must be understood that the enforcement depends ultimately upon action by the colonial Legislatures, and by the Imperial Ministers whose departments they concern. In addition to the Australasian naval arrangements, by which the Australasian contributions are to be largely increased on condition that certain vessels be officered and manned entirely by Australasians, a general increase in colonial naval subsidies was agreed to.

The scheme also provides that some colonies shall allot part of their local military forces to imperial defence in case of emergency but Canada and Australia contented themselves with agreeing to keep their local forces in a state of efficiency, relying on volunteers in case of imperial need as was done in the case of South Africa.

The contribution of Cape Colony to the Imperial navy was fixed at $250,000 annually, and Natal's at $175,000.

The preferential tariff arrangement is in a nebulous condition, depending entirely on future arrangements between the mother country and each individual colony, the understanding being that such arrangements would follow the general lines of the Canadian tariff.

The foregoing arrangements do not represent the unanimous opinion of the conference, but each resolution was adopted by a majority vote.

## 14 THE IMPERIALISTS: THE REAL ENEMIES OF EMPIRE BUILDING.

*The Manitoba Free Press, Winnipeg*
*August 14, 1902*

The conference of Colonial Premiers at London is now over. The results of the gathering are not known as yet, except in a general way; they are to be made public in a series of resolutions which are to be published with certain other cognate matters as a Parliamentary Blue Book. But it is perfectly well understood that nothing of a very revolutionary nature was decided upon; and in this fact lies the hope that the conference will prove of benefit to the empire. It is the rushers, the hustlers, the men who are for reducing all sections of the empire to a common denominator and merging them into a single figure that are the real enemies of Empire building. The great cause of a unified empire has ten times more reason to fear the labours of the George Parkins, the George Denisons and the Richard Seddons than any lukewarmness within or combination of hostile powers without.

---

## 15 CANADA'S REMOTENESS FROM WAR

*The Herald, Montreal*
*September 4, 1902*
[*quoted in The Canadian Annual Review,*
*1902, p.193*]

Dundonald[1] apparently shares a delusion dear to Hutton. He seems to think that the people of Canada are concerned about being in readiness for war, or if they are not they are to blame and should be stirred up. Any man who thinks that way—and all European soldiers do—fails to grasp the essential distinction between Europe and North America. With Europe war is a condition. With us it is a theory.

[1]Lord Dundonald was General Officer commanding the Canadian Militia.

---

## 16 LAURIER OFFERED AND RECEIVED NOTHING

*The Star, Montreal*
*November 4, 1902*

Laurier was partly responsible for the lack of progress at the Colonial Conference of 1902.

The Blue Book on the Colonial Conference issued in London yesterday shows that so far as practical results are concerned the conference was a failure. The report also throws some light on the reasons for its non-success.

The Canadian representatives came back from London empty-handed partly because they went there empty-handed, and partly because of the ambiguity of their position with regard to all the important issues before the conference.

The record shows that they did make a substantial offer of preferential treatment upon British goods coming into Canada in return for the exemption of Canadian products from duties imposed hereafter upon such products entering England. Unfortunately however their position was greatly weakened by two considerations. In the first place the United Kingdom was already in enjoyment of almost all the advantage that Canada had to offer, that is to say the preference of 33-1/3 per cent. In the second place all the public declarations of the Canadian Government and its press representatives were against the principle of the bargain proposed by the Ministers at the conference. They had denounced such an arrangement as equally undesirable and impossible as likely to be injurious to Canada and fatal to England. The 33-1/3 per cent preference was described as grateful tribute from Canada to the Mother country, free from all sordid considerations of self-interest.

---

## 17 A BRITISH CRITIC OF CANADA'S POSITION

*The Star, Montreal*
*January 21, 1903*

Sir John Colomb is again attacking Canada on account of the Dominion's attitude in regard to Imperial defence, and says in the *Morning Post* (London, England) today (January 21):

"Australia is far in advance of Canada in recognizing its duty to the fleet. The Dominion flatly refuses to give a penny though possessing a mercantile marine nearly equal to that of the United States, and is never tired urging on the mother country to undertake great cash subscriptions on finance guarantees to carry out transmarine schemes peculiar to the advantage of her own commercial interests."

## 18 CANADA SHOULD MEET CHAMBERLAIN HALFWAY

*The Star, Montreal*
*May 18, 1903*

When Joseph Chamberlain came out for an imperial preferential tariff scheme it was warmly welcomed by many in Canada especially the Conservatives.

Mr. R. L. Borden has cordially welcomed Mr. Chamberlain's great speech in favour of preferential trade within the Empire. Indeed, in view of his record and the record of his party which he leads, it is difficult to see how he could have done otherwise. The speech at Birmingham is the first definite and unqualified acceptance by a British statesman of the first rank of an Imperial policy suggested and advocated by the Conservative Party of Canada....

Canadians will naturally and very properly look at this question first from a Canadian point of view. That it will pay Canada to make very liberal commercial arrangements with the rest of the Empire while materially strengthening its protective walls against the nations not so friendly disposed towards the Dominion is the belief of the Conservative leaders at least.

Let us meet American hostility and German hostility with a protective tariff high enough to protect and let us make it worth the while of the Mother country to grant us discriminatory advantages as will make Canada the most profitable country in the world for the farmer. There is really no reason in the world why the political parties in Canada should be divided on this issue. We commend the idea to Sir Wilfrid and Mr. Fielding.

## 19 CAUTION IS ADVISED

*The Globe, Toronto*
*May 18, 1903*

Chamberlain receives the qualified support of some English Canadian Liberals.

So far as Canadians are concerned, no immediate action of a decisive kind is likely to be taken. Another year must elapse before any reduction in the preference can be proposed as a practical measure, and meanwhile much may happen as the result of an active protectionist propaganda, which is to be at once organized as the outcome of the deputation to Mr. Balfour. The people of this country will in general refrain from asking the people of Great Britain to tax themselves for the promotion of Imperial trade, but it is quite certain that if our friends across the Atlantic choose to grant such a preference as Mr. Chamberlain suggests it will be freely appreciated in Canada. In a very short time the food production of the Dominion will be adequate to meet the whole needs of the mother country, a change in the situation which cannot be ignored in the final determination of Imperial trade policy, as solving some of the problems involved.

## 20 THE PROTECTIONIST POSITION

*The News, Toronto*
*June 9, 1903*

Protectionist opposition to any extension of Canadian tariff preferences to the United Kingdom.

The attitude of the colonies toward an Imperial tariff is no more certain than that of the Mother Country. It is clear that Mr. Chamberlain looks for lower colonial tariffs on British manufactures. It is just as clear that the colonies are eager to develop their own industries and greatly concerned in the revenues which accrue from customs duties. In Canada we have had twenty-five years of protection, and many of our chief industries are established upon a protectionist basis. Except New South Wales, protection was the economic creed of all the Australasian colonies. The new southern Commonwealth has adopted a protectionist tariff, and seems unwilling to concede better treatment to British manufacturers, except in so far as this can be accomplished by higher duties against foreign countries. It is admitted that the Cape Colony has no enthusiasm for Mr. Chamberlain's policy. The other British South African States and New Zealand may go at least as far as Canada towards an Imperial zollverein. How far Canada will go has still to be determined. It is known that the Laurier Administration, in return for preferential treatment by Great Britain, is pledged to reduce still further the Canadian imposts on certain British manufactures, notwithstanding that some of our important industries now profess to be seriously injured by British competition. A union of Imperialism and tariff reform may make a formidable platform for Western Canada, but it is certain that any substantial steps towards lower duties will provoke resolute opposition in the industrial Provinces.

---

## 21  THE EMPIRE DOES NOT LIVE BY BREAD ALONE

*The Globe, Toronto*
*June 15, 1903*

Imperial unity is not based upon material considerations: Canada must proceed with great care.

There is one note in the Imperialist propaganda that rather jars on the ear of people whose sympathies nevertheless are warmly engaged for British connection. We mean the assumption that unless it is made worth their while to stay in the Empire the Colonies will drift away. At the Electrical Engineers Dinner Col. Denison seemed to adopt this view and told the assembled guests that unless preferential trade were granted the Empire would be "dissolved into separate atoms". That is

not a wholly noble view to take of the relations between colonies and mother country....

... If mutual material benefits can be added to mutual admiration and esteem, well and good. But we are venturing with a most delicate freight on an unknown sea. The first consequence seems to be that the fine feeling that now inspires the kinsmen on both sides of the ocean will be submitted to the hurly burly of a general election in Britain. The country will be divided and it will be made to appear that the English working man is to be asked to pay more for his bread in order that his dear brother in the colonies, who he has been told is much richer and fatter than he is, may get more for what he has to sell. If he votes against it and gets beaten, the fact will still remain that a fellow-Imperialist, who is now our sincere admirer, may have implanted in his mind a natural prejudice that, the prosperous children over the water have worked on the affections of the old fatherland and have secured a very good thing for themselves. On the other hand, if the party opposed to dear bread wins a decisive victory, will there not be a feeling of pique in the colonies, which if put into words would read: Well they are not ready to do much for us after all? And the feelings of brotherly love, which now exist clear as a mirror, will be breathed upon and dimmed. Is it not worth the while of our Imperialists to consider this aspect of the question, or a day may otherwise come when they will say, why did we not leave well enough alone? We should move very warily at least.

---

## 22  THE CANADIAN MANUFACTURERS' VIEW OF PREFERENTIAL TRADE

*The Manitoba Free Press, Winnipeg*
*October 12, 1903*

Chamberlain resigned from the British government in September 1903, but the debate on his proposals continued. Here western Liberals attack the Canadian Manufacturers Association and the Conservatives as the real enemies of Mr. Chamberlain.

They want the present British preference wiped out. But Mr. Chamberlain's policy is that in return for preferential treatment of our food products in Great Britain, we should allow the products of Great Britain's industry, of which the cotton industry is one of the most important, to enter our country upon terms which would enable the British manufacturer to sell not less but more of their goods in Canada than they do at present. The most determined enemies of the Chamberlain policy are the gentlemen in this country who make up the membership of the Manufacturers' Association and their friends, the gentlemen who make up the Conservative Party in Parliament.

# 23  IMPERIAL RELATIONS SERIOUSLY DAMAGED

*The Star, Montreal*
*October 21, 1903*

The announcement of the Alaska Boundary Award in October 1903 created great resentment in Canada against the British government and Lord Alverstone their appointee on the board.

London, October 21. A Canadian who has been intimately and prominently associated with the Alaska case, said: "It is the hardest blow the Imperial tie has ever received. The place Lord Alverstone filled was clearly that of agent for the British Government. It will be a shock to the Canadian people, notwithstanding all the professions of friendship and sympathy, the solemn formalities of the international court have simply been used for the purpose of handing over Canadian territory to the United States. Canada has been not only spontaneous but zealous, in defence of British territory and has not hesitated to sacrifice blood and treasure in defence of the motherland. She must now face the fact that when Imperial interests or friendship require it her territory may be handed over without the slightest hesitation. This marks a most serious epoch in the relations between Canada and the Mother Country."

# 24  BRITISH "STOOL-PIGEONS" AT WASHINGTON

*The Globe, Toronto*
*October 26, 1903*

Canadians will not be treated like children by the British Foreign Office. Canada may have to assume new powers within the empire to defend her rights against the actions of America's British "stool pigeons". With this event much of the emotional rhetoric and idealistic talk of imperial unity comes to a halt. The high noon of empire and imperialism had passed.

When Sir Wilfrid Laurier declared that Canada must petition for the right to negotiate her own treaties he came to the only conclusion that can be arrived at by anyone who reviews the situation dispassionately. It is idle to tell us that we did not have a good case when we feel that no matter how good our case might have been it would be rejected. What gives us legitimate cause for resentment is that we have been treated throughout like mere children. . . .

We in Canada believe that if the last backbone had been exhibited by the British Foreign Office the United States would have had to consent to a real arbitration or else be put in a position never to have the effrontery to talk about arbitration again. But the fact is that the main business of the British Minister at Washington is to act as stool-pigeon for the United States when any Canadian subject is up for negotiation.

# 25  CHAMBERLAIN: A GREAT COLONIAL SECRETARY

*The Globe, Toronto*
*November 20, 1903*

A Canadian comment on Joseph Chamberlain's career as Colonial Secretary, 1895-1903.

One does not need to agree with Mr. Chamberlain's fiscal views to recognize that he has been a constant and powerful friend of the lands across the seas. Lord Strathcona and the Agents General of the Colonies when taking official leave of Mr. Chamberlain could scarcely therefore exaggerate the sense of loss that his absence from the Colonial Office must create. In his present campaign he makes it abundantly plain that the good of the Colonies is as much in his mind as that of the Mother Country. This campaign may be difficult, etc. But whatever the result may be, there will have been a great awakening of thought, a renewed examination of things that were considered settled, endorsed and filed away forever. It will have been brought hence to men's minds that the Empire is concerned with the present and the future of many lands, many peoples and that it presents great problems which statesmen cannot ignore, but for which they must soon seek solutions. Mr. Chamberlain's name will be embalmed in a greater movement than the fiscal agitation and his part in that greater movement will be deemed that of a pioneer and discoverer.

# Appendix I

## The American Influences on Canadian Journalism and Literature

*The Canadian Magazine,*
*November 1898*

If there is one feature more than any other which is to be condemned in Canadian newspapers, it is their ceaseless quotation
from United States periodicals. A certain daily in British Columbia
has five or six columns a day of material which looks as if it were
clipped without change from United States dailies. In fact, in
reading some of the headings and opening paragraphs one gets
confused as to whether the paper is published in Canada or the
United States. A weekly published in Summerside, Prince Edward
Island, came to hand last week with nearly four columns of its front
page filled with quotations from New York magazines; one extract
was headed: "Our Military Mismanagement and Its Cause," and
yet it dealt with the Santiago campaign. These are but two of the
many examples which our newspaperdom offers.

Numbers of papers throughout the country use half-printed papers
technically known as ready-prints, or plate-matter prepared in
Toronto. The factories which produce these do not pay for their
contributed articles, stories and general matter. All this class of
reading is cut from the United States periodicals—practically stolen.
The weekly newspaper that uses such material cannot be highly
commended, and yet hundreds of weeklies do use it in every issue.

As citizens, we often lament the slow growth of patriotism and of
Canadian literature. And is this slowness of growth surprising
when our newspapers make no difference between what is foreign
and what is Canadian; when journalists do not think it improper
to call the United States military problems "our problems"; when
United States school books are designated "our school books" by
these intelligent wielders of the scissors; when Canadian short-
story writers are ignored, and United States litterateurs boomed
and advertised; when Canadian poets and writers are snubbed and
foreigners exalted to the seats of fame?

And the journalists of the country are no more careless than the people, or this state of circumstances would not exist. If Canadians demanded Canadian literature they would get it. But they buy United States books, United States magazines, United States periodicals at higher prices than are asked for good native material; and even admitting for the sake of argument that this United States material is better than corresponding Canadian reading, there is little excuse for such conduct. Canadian journalists and Canadian readers owe a duty to themselves and to their country, the sense of which should be strong enough to insist that Canadian literature should have first place on their reading tables and on their bookshelves.

Then there comes up the question of British newspapers and books. We seldom see a quotation from a British newspaper in a Canadian daily, unless it is in the cable despatches, and ninety-five per cent of these cables come through New York. Nor do the people. There are ten United States monthlies and weeklies sold in Canada to one British periodical. And yet we pride ourselves on our British connection; we revere the Union Jack and all it represents; and we bow down and worship the god-like Mother, who is a pattern of goodness and virtue to all her people.

# Appendix II

## Yellow Journalism and Government Ownership of the Canadian press

*The Canadian Magazine,*
*November 1900*

Millionaires with a feverish desire to make more millions out of building and running railways are driving us to advocate Government ownership of these trade servers. Mr. Harmsworth, the millionaire proprietor of the London Daily Mail, is now endeavouring to buy the London Times, the most stable organ of public opinion in the world. Mr. Harmsworth and his imitators, for he is sure to have imitators, must be careful or Government ownership of newspapers will be a live topic. Already the signs point that way. Democracy is suffering from the irresponsible and unreliable daily papers which, like strong drink, tend to inflame men's passions. Some people in London are proposing that the British Parliament shall pass legislation providing penalties for the publication of incorrect and unreliable and extravagant news. This is the result of the publication in London of sensational stories from China which never came over the cable.

Apropos of this, it is said that a certain Canadian daily paper published some half-dozen cablegrams from its war correspondent in South Africa, which the correspondent declared, on his return, to have been forgeries. Another Canadian daily is in the habit of publishing "expanded" cablegrams from foreign storm-centres which have not always been based upon genuine cablegrams. If punishment follows in the form of a new kind of censorship, the newspaper publishers will have only themselves to blame. A reaction against foolish sensationalism, and the steady growth of education among the common people, may however cause a reaction rendering such legislation unnecessary; but the indications do not point that way.

# Canadian Weeklies and Monthlies
## Mentioned in this Volume

| PAPER | POLITICS | CIRCULATION |
|---|---|---|
| **NOVA SCOTIA** | | |
| *L'Évangéline,* Weymouth | French language weekly | 2,000 |
| **QUEBEC** | | |
| *La Vérité,* Quebec City | ultramontane religious weekly | unknown |
| *Le Monde,* Montreal | illustrated weekly | 2,200? |
| *L'Interprète,* Montebello | weekly | unknown |
| **ONTARIO** | | |
| *The Canadian Churchman,* Toronto | Anglican weekly | 2,500 |
| *The Canadian Magazine,* Toronto | Monthly | 20,500 |
| *The Methodist Magazine and Review,* Toronto | Methodist weekly | 2,900 |
| *The Monetary Times,* Toronto | Financial weekly | 6,000 |
| *The Orange Sentinel,* Toronto | Orange Order weekly | 4,000 |
| *The Weekly Sun,* Toronto | Goldwin Smith's agrarian protest weekly | 15,500 |
| **BRITISH COLUMBIA** | | |
| *The Province,* Victoria | weekly to 1898 | unknown |

The circulation and the other data in the above chart drawn from A. McKim *The Canadian Newspaper Directory, 1899*. Montreal: McKim Advertising Agency, 1899, and *The American Newspaper Directory, 1901:* New York: Geo. P. Rowell and Co., 1901. The latter covers all the provinces of Canada.

# A Guide to Journals of Canada in 1901

| PAPER | POLITICS | CIRCULATION |
|---|---|---|
| **NOVA SCOTIA** | | |
| *The News*, Amherst | Independent | unknown |
| *The Press*, Amherst | Conservative | unknown |
| *The Acadian Record*, Halifax | Liberal | 3,000 |
| *The Chronicle*, Halifax | Liberal | 5,000 |
| *The Echo (Ev Chronicle)*, Halifax | Liberal | 4,000 |
| *The Herald*, Halifax | Conservative | 5,050 |
| *The Mail*, Halifax | Conservative | 4,100 |
| *The Post*, Sydney | Conservative | unknown |
| *The Record*, Sydney | Liberal | unknown |
| *The News*, Truro | Independent | 500 |
| | | |
| **PRINCE EDWARD ISLAND** | | |
| *The Examiner*, Charlottetown | Conservative | 1,150 |
| *The Guardian*, Charlottetown | Independent | 1,150 |
| *The Patriot*, Charlottetown | Liberal | 750 |
| | | |
| **NEW BRUNSWICK** | | |
| *The Gleaner*, Fredericton | Conservative | 1,950 |
| *The Herald*, Fredericton | Liberal | 750 |
| *The Times*, Moncton | Conservative | 1,000 |
| *The Transcript*, Moncton | Liberal | 1,000 |
| *The Gazette*, Saint John | Conservative | 3,750 |
| *The Globe*, Saint John | Liberal | 4,000 |
| *The Star*, Saint John | Conservative | unknown |
| *The Sun*, Saint John | Conservative | 3,900 |
| *The Telegraph*, Saint John | Liberal | 3,000 |
| | | |
| **QUEBEC** | | |
| *Quotidien*, Levis | Independent | unknown |
| *The Gazette*, Montreal | Conservative | 9,200 |
| *The Herald*, Montreal | Liberal | unknown |
| *Le Journal*, Montreal | Conservative | unknown |
| *La Patrie*, Montreal | Liberal | 19,650 |
| *La Presse*, Montreal | Liberal | 63,200 |
| *The Star*, Montreal | Conservative | 52,600 |
| *The Witness*, Montreal | Independent | 13,975 |

| | | |
|---|---|---:|
| *The Chronicle*, Quebec | Conservative | 3,100 |
| *L'Événement*, Quebec | Independent | 8,500 |
| *Le Soleil*, Quebec | Liberal | 6,500 |
| *The Mercury*, Quebec | Conservative | 1,000 |
| *The Telegraph*, Quebec | Independent | 2,800 |
| *L'Union*, St. Hyacinthe | Liberal | 1,000 |
| *The Record*, Sherbrooke | Independent | 2,375 |

## ONTARIO

| | | |
|---|---|---:|
| *The Intelligencer*, Belleville | Conservative | 800 |
| *Ontario*, Belleville | Liberal | 750 |
| *The News-Record*, Berlin | Conservative | 1,250 |
| *The Telegraph*, Berlin | Liberal | 500 |
| *The Courier*, Brantford | Conservative | 2,000 |
| *The Expositor*, Brantford | Liberal | 3,100 |
| *The Recorder*, Brockville | Liberal | 1,300 |
| *The Times*, Brockville | Conservative | 1,000 |
| *The Banner News*, Chatham | Liberal | 1,750 |
| *The Planet*, Chatham | Conservative | 1,000 |
| *The Times-Journal*, Fort William | Independent | unknown |
| *The Reformer*, Galt | Liberal | 1,100 |
| *The Reporter*, Galt | Conservative | 1,000 |
| *The Herald*, Guelph | Conservative | 1,000 |
| *The Mercury*, Guelph | Liberal | 1,550 |
| *The Herald*, Hamilton | Independent | 6,000 |
| *The Morning Post*, Hamilton | Conservative | unknown |
| *The Spectator*, Hamilton | Conservative | 7,500 |
| *The Times*, Hamilton | Liberal | 5,250 |
| *The Chronicle*, Ingersoll | Liberal | 500 |
| *The British Whig*, Kingston | Liberal | 2,600 |
| *The News*, Kingston | Conservative | 1,500 |
| *The Times*, Kingston | Independent | 1,560 |
| *The Post*, Lindsay | Conservative | 500 |
| *The Advertiser*, London | Liberal | 6,500 |
| *The Free Press*, London | Conservative | 7,750 |
| *The News*, London | Independent | 8,300 |
| *The Record*, Niagara Falls | Conservative | unknown |
| *The Citizen*, Ottawa | Conservative | unknown |
| *The Free Press*, Ottawa | Liberal | 5,400 |
| *The Journal*, Ottawa | Independent | 7,150 |
| *Le Temps*, Ottawa | Liberal | 2,300 |
| *The Examiner*, Peterborough | Liberal | 1,250 |
| *The Review*, Peterborough | Conservative | 750 |
| *The Times*, Peterborough | Independent | unknown |
| *The Guide*, Port Hope | Liberal | 500(?) |
| *Lake of the Woods*, Rat Portage | Independent | unknown |
| *The Journal*, St. Catharines | Liberal | 1,250 |
| *The Standard*, St. Catharines | Conservative | 1,500 |
| *The Star*, St. Catharines | Conservative | 1,000 |

| | | |
|---|---|---|
| *The Journal*, St. Thomas | Liberal | 3,175 |
| *The Times*, St. Thomas | Conservative | 2,800 |
| *The Observer*, Sarnia | Liberal | unknown |
| *The Beacon*, Stratford | Liberal | 750 |
| *The Herald*, Stratford | Conservative | 875 |
| *The Globe*, Toronto | Liberal | 34,800 |
| *The Mail and Empire*, Toronto | Conservative | 29,150 |
| *The News*, Toronto | Conservative | 42,300 |
| *The Star*, Toronto | Liberal | 15,000 |
| *The Telegram*, Toronto | Independent | 24,100 |
| *The World*, Toronto | Conservative | 25,100 |
| *The Record*, Windsor | Liberal | 1,500 |
| *The Express*, Woodstock | Conservative | 750 |
| *The Review Sentinel*, Woodstock | Liberal | 2,650 |
| *The Times*, Woodstock | Conservative | 1,500 |

## MANITOBA

| | | |
|---|---|---|
| *The Sun*, Brandon | Liberal | 530 |
| *The News*, Dauphin | Independent | unknown |
| *The Graphic*, Portage La Prairie | Independent | unknown |
| *The News*, Portage La Prairie | Conservative | unknown |
| *The Manitoba Free Press*, Winnipeg | Liberal | 11,400 |
| *The Telegram*, Winnipeg | Conservative | 3,500 |
| *The Tribune*, Winnipeg | Independent | 6,500 |

## NORTH WESTERN TERRITORIES

| | | |
|---|---|---|
| *The Herald*, Calgary | Independent | 650 |

## BRITISH COLUMBIA

| | | |
|---|---|---|
| *The Times*, Greenwood | Independent | unknown |
| *The Free Press*, Nanaimo | Independent | 500 |
| *The Miner*, Nelson | Independent | 500 |
| *The Tribune*, Nelson | Independent | unknown |
| *The Columbian*, New Westminster | Independent | 750 |
| *The Evening World*, Rossland | Labour | unknown |
| *The Miner*, Rossland | Independent | unknown |
| *The News-Advertiser*, Vancouver | Independent | 2,250 |
| *The Province*, Vancouver[1] | Liberal | 4,300 |
| *The World*, Vancouver | Liberal | 3,175 |
| *The Colonist*, Victoria | Conservative | 3,000 |
| *The Times*, Victoria | Liberal | 2,750 |

## YUKON

| | | |
|---|---|---|
| *The Journal*, Dawson City | Independent | unknown |
| *The News*, Dawson City | Independent | unknown |
| *The Nugget*, Dawson City | Independent | unknown |
| *The Yukon Sun*, Dawson City | Liberal | unknown |

[1]The Victoria *Province* (a weekly) became the Vancouver *Province* (a daily) in 1898.

# For Further Reading

Annett, D. R.      *British Preference in Canadian Commercial Policy*. Toronto: The Ryerson Press, 1948.

Berger, Carl      *The Sense of Power*. Toronto: University of Toronto Press, 1970.

Berger, Carl      *Imperialism and Nationalism, 1884-1914*. Toronto: University of Toronto Press, 1969.

Bourassa, Henri      *Great Britain and Canada*. Montreal: Beauchemin, 1901.

Burnham, J. H.      *Canadians in the Imperial Naval and Military Service Abroad*. Toronto: Williamson, 1891.

Brown, R. C.      *Canada's National Policy, 1883-1900*. Princeton: Princeton University Press, 1964.

Brown, S. M.      *With the Royal Canadians*. Toronto: Publishers' Syndicate, 1900.

Denison, G. T.      *The Struggle for Imperial Unity*. Toronto: Macmillan, 1909.

Duncan, S. J.      *The Imperialist*. Reprint, Toronto: New Canadian Library, 1961.

Evans, W. S.      *The Canadian Contingents and Canadian Imperialism*. Toronto: Publishers' Syndicate, 1900.

Ewart, J. S.      *The Kingdom of Canada, and other Essays*. Toronto: Morang, 1908.

Kendle, J. E.      *The Colonial and Imperial Conferences, 1887-1911*. London: Longmans, 1967.

Levitt, Joseph      *Henri Bourassa on Imperialism and Bi-Culturalism*. Toronto: Copp Clark, 1970.

MacLean, G. R.      *The Imperial Federation Movement in Canada*. unpublished Ph.D. thesis, Duke University, 1958.

McKim, A.      *The Canadian Newspaper Directory, 1899*. Montreal: McKim Advertising Agency, 1899.

Morrison, E. W. B.    *With the Guns in South Africa.* Hamilton:
                      Spectator Printing Company, 1901.

Neatby, H. B.        "Laurier and Imperialism," *Canadian Historical
                     Association Annual Report, 1955.* Toronto: University of
                     Toronto Press, 1956, pp. 24-32.

O'Connell, M. P.     "The Ideas of Henri Bourassa," *Canadian Journal of
                     Economics and Political Science,* XIX, 3
                     (August, 1953), 361-376.

Ollivier, M.         *The Colonial and Imperial Conferences,* Vol. I. Ottawa:
                     The Queen's Printer, 1954.

Page, R. J. D.       "Canada and the Imperial Idea in the Boer War Years,"
                     *Journal of Canadian Studies,* V, 1 (February, 1970),
                     33-49.

Penlington, N.       *Canada and Imperialism, 1896-1899.* Toronto:
                     University of Toronto Press, 1965.

Preston, R. A.       *Canada and "Imperial Defense."* Durham:
                     Duke University Press, 1967.

Smith, Goldwin       *In the Court of History, An Apology for those Canadians
                     who were opposed to the War in South Africa.* Toronto:
                     William Tyrrell Company, 1902.

Smith, Goldwin       *Canada and the Canadian Question.* Toronto: Hunter Rose,
                     1891.